YORK NOTES

JANE EYRE

CHARLOTTE BRONTË

NOTES BY SARAH ROWBOTHAM

 Longman

York Press

The right of Sarah Rowbotham to be identified as Author
of this Work has been asserted by her in accordance with
the Copyright, Designs and Patents Act 1988

YORK PRESS
322 Old Brompton Road, London SW5 9JH

PEARSON EDUCATION LIMITED
Edinburgh Gate, Harlow,
Essex CM20 2JE, United Kingdom
Associated companies, branches and representatives throughout the world

First published 1997
This new and fully revised edition first published 2002

10 9 8 7 6 5 4 3 2 1

ISBN 0–582–50621–2

Designed by Michelle Cannatella
Illustrated by Tony Chance
Typeset by Land & Unwin (Data Sciences), Bugbrooke, Northamptonshire
Produced by Addison Wesley Longman China Limited, Hong Kong

CONTENTS

PART ONE
INTRODUCTION

How to study a novel 5
Author and context 6
Setting and background 8
Character tree 9
Timeline 10

PART TWO
SUMMARIES

General summary 12

Detailed summaries
Chapters 1–4 14
Chapters 5–10 20
Chapters 11–27 28
Chapters 28–35 51
Chapters 36–8 62

PART THREE
COMMENTARY

Themes 67
Structure 72
Characters 73
Language and style 80

PART FOUR
RESOURCES

How to use quotations 84
Coursework essay 85
Sitting the examination 86
Improve your grade 87
Sample essay plan 91
Further questions 92

LITERARY TERMS 94

CHECKPOINT HINTS/ANSWERS 95

TEST ANSWERS 97

PREFACE

York Notes are designed to give you a broader perspective on works of literature studied at GCSE and equivalent levels. With examination requirements changing in the twenty-first century, we have made a number of significant changes to this new series. We continue to help students to reach their own interpretations of the text but York Notes now have important extra-value new features.

You will discover that York Notes are genuinely interactive. The new **Checkpoint** features make sure that you can test your knowledge and broaden your understanding. You will also be directed to excellent websites, books and films where you can follow up ideas for yourself.

The **Resources** section has been updated and an entirely new section has been devoted to how to improve your grade. Careful reading and application of the principles laid out in the Resources section guarantee improved performance.

The **Detailed summaries** include an easy-to-follow skeleton structure of the story-line, while the section on **Language and style** has been extended to offer an in-depth discussion of the writer's techniques.

The Contents page shows the structure of this study guide. However, there is no need to read from the beginning to the end as you would with a novel, play or poem. Use the Notes in the way that suits you. Our aim is to help you with your understanding of the work, not to dictate how you should learn.

Our authors are practising English teachers and examiners who have used their experience to offer a whole range of **Examiner's secrets** – useful hints to encourage exam success.

The General Editor of this series is John Polley, Senior GCSE Examiner and former Head of English at Harrow Way Community School, Andover.

The author of these Notes, Sarah Rowbotham, is currently an English examiner for one of the largest examination bodies. She is Head of English at a comprehensive school in Sheffield. Her previous York Notes titles are *Nineteenth Century Short Stories*, *Much Ado About Nothing* and *Emma*. She is also the author of the York Personal Tutor on *Shakespeare*.

The text used in these Notes is the new Penguin Classics edition, published 1996, edited by Micheal Mason.

INTRODUCTION

HOW TO STUDY A NOVEL

A novelist starts with a story that examines a situation and the actions of particular characters. Remember that authors are not photographers, and that a novel never resembles real life exactly. Ultimately, a novel represents a view of the world that has been created in the author's imagination.

There are six features of a novel:

1 THE STORY: this is the series of events, deliberately organised by the writer to test the characters

2 THE CHARACTERS: the people who have to respond to the events of the story. Since they are human, they can be good or bad, clever or stupid, likeable or detestable, etc. They may change too!

3 THE VIEWPOINT/VOICE: who is telling the story. The viewpoint may come from one of the characters, or from an omniscient (all-seeing) narrator, which allows the novelist to write about the perspectives of all the characters

4 THE THEMES: these are the underlying messages, or meanings, of the novel

5 THE SETTING: this concerns the time and place that the author has chosen for the story

6 THE LANGUAGE AND STYLE: these are the words that the author has used to influence our understanding of the novel

To arrive at the fullest understanding of a novel, you need to read it several times. In this way, you can see how all the choices the author has made add up to a particular view of life, and develop your own ideas about it.

The purpose of these York Notes is to help you understand what the novel is about and to enable you to make your own interpretation. Do not expect the study of a novel to be neat and easy: novels are chosen for examination purposes, not written for them!

www. CHECK THE NET
www.victorianweb .org has lots of information on Charlotte Brontë and her works

AUTHOR – LIFE AND WORKS	CONTEXT
	1815 Napoleon becomes Emperor and is defeated at Waterloo
1816 Birth of Charlotte Brontë	**1816** Jane Austen's *Emma* is published
1817 Birth of Charlotte's brother, Branwell Brontë	**1817** Jane Austen dies
1818 Charlotte's sister, Emily, is born	
1819 The Brontë family move to Haworth in Yorkshire	
1820 Anne Brontë is born	**1820** George III dies, and George IV becomes king
1821 Charlotte Brontë's mother dies of cancer	**1821** John Keats dies
1824 Two of Charlotte's sisters, Maria and Elizabeth, die of tuberculosis at Cowan Bridge School	**1824** Lord Byron dies
	1825 First railway opened between Stockton and Darlington
	1830 George IV dies and is succeeded by William IV
1831 Charlotte boards at Roe Head School, Mirfield	**1831** Cholera epidemic
	1832 Walter Scott dies; First Reform Act
	1833 Slavery abolished
	1834 Tolpuddle martyrs
1835 Charlotte returns to Roe Head as a teacher; initially, her sister Emily is a pupi	**1837** William IV dies, and Queen Victoria comes to the throne
	1838 'People's Charter' published
1839 Charlotte, now a governess, turns down two proposals of marriage	**1839** Chartist petition rejected by Parliament; riots in Birmingham
1841 Charlotte becomes governess to a family near Bradford	**1840** Penny Post is established

AUTHOR – LIFE AND WORKS

1842 Charlotte and Emily study French in Brussels

1844 Charlotte returns home when her father becomes almost totally blind

1847 *Jane Eyre* is published under an author named Currer Bell. *Wuthering Heights* by Charlotte Brontë's sister, Emily, is published

1848 Charlotte's brother Branwell dies of alcoholism; her sister Emily dies of tuberculosis. *The Tenant of Wildfell Hall* by Charlotte Brontë's sister, Anne, is published

1849 Charlotte Brontë's sister Anne dies of tuberculosis; Charlotte publishes *Shirley*

1853 Charlotte Brontë publishes *Villette*, based on her experiences in Brussels

1854 Charlotte marries her father's curate, Arthur Nicholls

1855 Charlotte, who is pregnant, dies of pneumonia

CONTEXT

1842 Second Chartist petition presented and rejected

1845 Famine in Ireland due to potato blight

1848 Revolutions in Europe

1849 Cholera epidemic

1851 The Great Exhibition at Crystal Palace

1852 Harriet Beecher Stowe publishes *Uncle Tom's Cabin*

1854 Cholera epidemic in England

SETTING AND BACKGROUND

THE WEATHER

DID YOU KNOW?

Charlotte Brontë based Thornfield Hall on a real place she had visited as a governess.

The setting of *Jane Eyre* is vital to the plot and action, and often gives the reader an added dimension which helps our understanding of character and scene.

Consider the ways in which Charlotte Brontë involves the weather in the novel: there are numerous examples of climatic conditions intensifying mood (**pathetic fallacy**). The bleak view from the window in the opening section reinforces the idea of little Jane's unhappiness; 'a scene of wet lawn and storm-beat shrub, with ceaseless rain sweeping away wildly before a long and lamentable blast' (Ch. 1, p. 14). The freezing conditions at Lowood add to the misery there in the same way that the storm in the Thornfield orchard on the night of Rochester's proposal gives a feeling of foreboding.

Charlotte Brontë was very much influenced by writers of Gothic fiction, with its melodrama, haunted and gloomy castles, and innocent heroines. Thornfield is vaguely threatening with its sombre rooms hung with tapestry, its strange noises and mysterious secrets, and fits into this genre very well: 'I lingered in the long passage ... narrow, low, and dim, with only one little window at the far end ... like a corridor in some Bluebeard's castle' (Ch. 11, p. 122).

SURROUNDINGS

Houses and possessions are used to add information about characters. The Rivers are not wealthy and yet Jane approves of their home because it typifies the values of cleanliness and common sense:

'The parlour was rather a small room, very plainly furnished; yet comfortable, because clean and neat. The old-fashioned chairs were very bright, and the walnut-wood table was like a looking-glass ... everything – including the carpet and curtains – looked at once well worn and well saved'. (Ch. 29, p. 385)

She is much more at home in this kind of environment than at the grand houses of Gateshead or Thornfield, and it is logical that she and Rochester should eventually settle at Ferndean Manor which is much less imposing than Thornfield Hall.

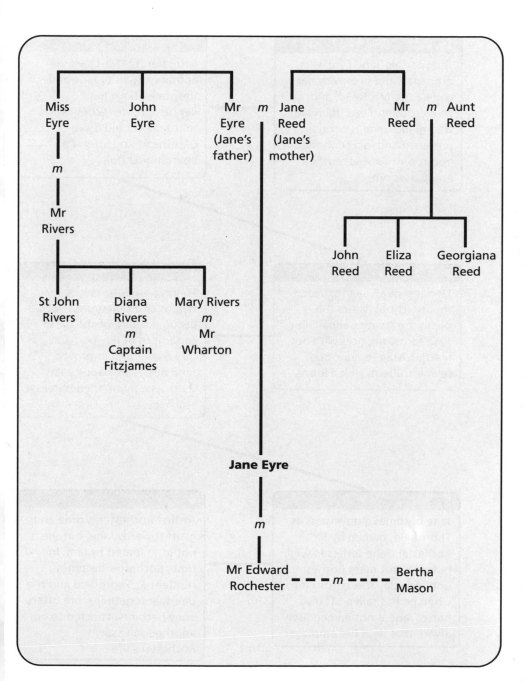

1

Ten-year-old Jane Eyre is orphaned and lives with her cruel aunt, Mrs Reed, and three cousins, Eliza, John and Georgiana. Jane is wrongly punished and locked in the 'red-room'. Jane is terrified and passes out.

2

After her 'fit' Mr Lloyd, an apothecary, visits Jane and they talk about her depression. He recommends that Jane should leave Gateshead and attend a boarding school.

3

Jane is sent away to Lowood charity school where the pupils are treated appallingly. Jane forms alliances with her teacher, Miss Temple, and fellow-student, Helen Burns.

4

There is an outbreak of typhus and Helen dies. People become aware of the harsh conditions at Lowood and it is taken over and improved. Jane passes six happy years there as a pupil, then two as a teacher.

5

Jane becomes a governess at Thornfield, owned by Mr Rochester. Jane settles in well, but does not meet Rochester until one day she assists him when he has fallen off his horse. Jane is not immediately aware that he is her employer.

6

At first Rochester is rude and gruff towards Jane, but she is not intimidated by him. In time, Rochester becomes resident at Thornfield and the pair talk together more often. They become attracted to one another. Jane saves Rochester's life.

7

Rochester leaves Thornfield for a while and returns with a rich and beautiful companion, Blanche Ingram. Jane becomes jealous when she believes they are to marry. Jane goes to see her dying aunt and Jane forgives her past behaviour.

8

When Jane returns, Rochester denies his engagement to Miss Ingram. Then, despite the differences in their age and status, Rochester asks Jane to marry him. Jane is very happy.

9

On the day of their wedding, Jane discovers that Rochester is already married. Rochester leads them to the house and reveals his wife, a mad woman who is being kept in the attic.

10

Jane refuses to be Rochester's mistress and leaves Thornfield. She is destitute and is saved by three people who turn out to be her cousins (Diana, Mary and St John). Jane becomes a teacher at a new local school and settles in to her new life.

11

Jane inherits some money from an uncle and shares it with her cousins. St John proposes marriage to Jane, even though he does not love her. He believes that she would be a good missionary's wife. Jane refuses as she still loves Rochester.

12

One night, Jane hears Rochester calling and returns to Thornfield. She discovers that Mrs Rochester has burned down the house and has died. Rochester has been maimed and blinded. The novel ends with his marriage to Jane and a description of the happy life ahead of them.

PART TWO

SUMMARIES

GENERAL SUMMARY

CHAPTERS 1–4: GATESHEAD – THE ORPHANED EARLY YEARS

DID YOU KNOW?

Many of the details of Jane Eyre's childhood are drawn from the author's own life.

Jane Eyre is an orphan. Both her parents have died within a year of her birth, leaving her to the care of an aunt, Mrs Reed of Gateshead. Mrs Reed is a widow, whose husband was the brother of Jane's mother. Before his death he made his wife promise to care for the child. Mrs Reed keeps her promise only narrowly: she feeds, clothes and houses the little girl. She resents her, however, and treats her cruelly. As the novel opens, Jane is ten years old, withdrawn and unloved, but high-spirited and with a strong sense of justice. She resents the harsh treatment from her aunt and cousins, and has severe temper outbursts, which shock and outrage Mrs Reed so much that she arranges for Jane to be sent away to school.

CHAPTERS 5–10: LOWOOD – SCHOOL

Jane spends eight years at Lowood, a charity boarding school. To start with it is a hard life. Living conditions are terrible: there is never enough food or heating, and many children become ill and die from typhus fever. Mr Brocklehurst, the head of the institution, is a cruel man whose misguided religious ideas about how to build character and feed the soul are soon criticised by the general population. The school is taken over by kinder people; and Jane flourishes under better conditions and sound teaching. She becomes one of the teachers herself, respected and loved, with a strong sense of personal integrity.

CHAPTERS 11–27: THORNFIELD – LIFE AND LOVE BEGIN

Aged eighteen, she seeks a job as governess in a private household. She comes to Thornfield, home of Mr Rochester and his ward. Mr Rochester, some twenty-five years older than her, returns home after a long absence. He meets and falls in love with Jane. Despite the difference in their social rank he wants to marry her. Just at the point when the fairytale is about to become reality – actually at the altar – the marriage is halted by an announcement that Mr Rochester already has a wife. This discovery of 'the madwoman in the attic' nearly destroys Jane along with her hopes of happiness. In spite of Mr Rochester's pleas and protestations and her devoted love for him, she will not agree to be his mistress. She flees Thornfield.

CHAPTERS 28–35: MARCH END – ADULTHOOD AND THE ROAD TO KNOWLEDGE

Penniless and almost starving, Jane wanders the countryside looking for work and food. She stumbles upon a house one night when she is just running out of strength. The occupants let her in and save her from death. St John, Diana and Mary Rivers look after her and they become her family. It turns out that they are in fact cousins. Jane receives an inheritance and insists on sharing it with them, allowing her to repay their kindness and enabling all four to become financially independent at last.

During Jane's long months away from Thornfield, Mr Rochester has never left her thoughts. She knows that whilst he has a wife living she can never be with him, and mourns the loss of their love deeply. St John proposes marriage and invites her to travel with him to India to be a missionary. She considers this, but the desire to be near Mr Rochester keeps her in England. One night, when she is being pressed by St John into making a decision, she 'hears' a voice crying for her in despair.

CHAPTERS 36–8: THE JOURNEY HOME

She returns to Thornfield, finding it a blackened ruin and the mad Mrs Rochester dead. She finds Mr Rochester, now blinded and partially crippled. The novel ends with their marriage and the prospect of a peaceful, contented life ahead.

DID YOU KNOW?

The words 'Reader, I married him' (Ch. 38, p. 498) are the most famous in the novel.

DETAILED SUMMARIES

CHAPTER 1 – Jane lets fly at Master John

① **Jane Eyre lives in a grand house with her aunt and cousins.**

② **She is unhappy and hides away to read.**

③ **Her cousin John discovers her and is abusive.**

④ **Jane is punished for her angry outburst by being locked in the 'red-room' (p. 18).**

? DID YOU KNOW?

Charlotte Brontë's mother, like Jane Eyre's, died when the author was very young.

At the opening of the novel Jane Eyre is ten years old. She is an orphan and lives in a very grand house with her aunt, Mrs Reed, and this lady's three children: Master John, Eliza and Georgiana. We quickly discover that Jane is a most unhappy little girl.

From the start her sense of loneliness and isolation is evident in the way she hides herself behind thick curtains in a deserted room, ostracised by her aunt and cousins. She muses on her relief that the weather is too inclement for any possibility of a walk, and spends her time studying a book, Bewick's *History of British Birds*, whose pictures fascinate her. Note how the pictures in the book add to the creation of mood.

When she is discovered there by cousin John, he is cruel and abusive to her. Her resulting anger and refusal to be dominated are severely punished – Mrs Reed declares, 'Take her away to the red-room, and lock her in there' (p. 18).

It is quickly clear that Jane has a strong personality and is beginning to question the behaviour and attitudes of those around her. Although young, she refuses to be dominated by her elder, male cousin; she recognises him for the bully that he is and stands up to his cruelty.

Her independence and strength of character is shown in well-defined opinions. Lashing out verbally and physically at cousin John is a sign of her strong nature and desire to be treated fairly.

The weather outside is cold, wet and miserable: 'near, a scene of wet lawn and storm-beat shrub, with ceaseless rain sweeping away wildly before a long and lamentable blast' (p. 14). There is pathetic fallacy in the reflection of Jane's situation in the miserable weather. Also the gloomy pictures in the book fascinate her as they also mirror her situation.

EXAMINER'S SECRET

A sign of a good candidate is the ability to cross-reference, e.g. provide evidence of Jane's independence from different parts of the novel.

CHAPTER 2 – The horrors of the red-room

❶ Jane is carried to the red-room.

❷ She is terrified in this room, where her uncle died.

❸ As it grows dark, she screams out.

❹ Mrs Reed refuses to let her leave the room.

❺ Jane passes out from terror.

Bessie and Abbot carry Jane to the red-room.

This is obviously a terrible punishment to inflict upon a little girl. She is clearly desperate and very afraid, but Mrs Reed has absolutely no sympathy for her. Seen through Jane's eyes she is clearly a cruel woman; however, even Jane admits that Mrs Reed sincerely believes that Jane is artful and wicked, therefore it is a just punishment in this lady's eyes.

DID YOU KNOW?

Charlotte Brontë was not the only writer in her family. Her sisters Emily and Anne were also novelists.

Jane's personality becomes clearer in this chapter; at ten years old she is able to look at her situation and judge it very honestly. She recognises that it is not her fault that she is being punished, and that her aunt and cousins resent her terribly for being an unwanted burden. She sees their cruelty and is very angry – '"Unjust! – unjust!" said my reason' (p. 22).

The red-room

The red-room is an old disused bedroom. It was here that Mrs Reed's husband, Jane's uncle, died some nine years before. Jane is clearly terrified about the prospect of being locked in this room with all its gloomy associations. (Note the author's use of descriptive language about the setting.) Initially she bears her punishment with fortitude. She is still extremely distressed and angry, and ponders on the unjust treatment she habitually receives from her family. She accepts that she is unwanted and unloved and does not fit in at Gateshead at all. As it begins to grow dark she becomes more aware and more afraid of her surroundings. She becomes convinced that the room is haunted and screams out for help. Although the servants come to her aid, they are unsympathetic, and Mrs Reed insists that Jane be thrust bodily back inside the room and the door locked behind her. At this point Jane faints – 'I suppose I had a species of fit' (p. 25) – in sheer terror.

An interesting interpretation of the 'red' room relates to the colour associations with anger – Jane's pent-up fury which is caused by her treatment at the hands of the Reeds.

CHAPTER 3 – Jane would like to go to school

1. Jane wakes up in her own bed.
2. She realises Bessie and Mr Lloyd are also there.
3. The apothecary comes back and questions her.
4. He recognises she is unhappy and should perhaps be sent away to school.

Jane wakes up in bed in the nursery, confused and afraid. Her 'fit' has left her weak and disorientated. Gradually she becomes aware that there are two people with her – Bessie and 'Mr Lloyd, an apothecary' (p. 26). Bessie is gentle and kind towards her, giving her many special treats. However, the miserable truth of her situation affects her so that all the kindness in the world will not cheer her spirits.

Mr Lloyd also treats her kindly. When he revisits her the next day he questions her closely about her obvious depression. As the narrator says, 'Children can feel, but they cannot analyse their feelings' (p. 31). However, Jane tells Mr Lloyd enough for him to recognise that she is unhappy at Gateshead and that to be sent away to school would benefit her greatly. Mr Lloyd concludes, 'The child ought to have a change of air and scene' (p. 33).

> **CHECKPOINT 1**
>
> How can we tell that the apothecary is sympathetic to Jane's situation?

The adult **narrator** Jane recognises the shrewdness in Mr Lloyd that the child does not understand. He clearly agrees that her treatment at Gateshead is harsh and unfair, and is trying to help her by suggesting the idea of school.

Jane is very aware of her weak and unappealing features, and how she is unfavourably compared to Miss Georgiana (p. 34). However, rather than accepting this, there is an implicit sense of her reacting very strongly to the unfairness of such a surface judgement. The **theme** of being judged and consequently rewarded or punished in life because of physical appearances begins to be addressed in this chapter.

CHAPTER 4 – Mr Brocklehurst, and a battle with Aunt Reed

1. Jane waits for news about going to school.
2. She is not included in the family's Christmas celebrations.
3. Jane hits John when he tries to bully her.
4. Mr Brocklehurst arrives to talk of school.
5. Jane and Mrs Reed have a final row.

> **GLOSSARY**
>
> apothecary medical practitioner licensed to give medicine but inferior to doctor

Although Jane knows that Mr Lloyd has suggested school to Mrs Reed, she waits in vain for any further news on the subject. Christmas

Chapter 4 continued

comes and goes – a terrible time for any child who is unloved and unwanted. She is excluded from all the celebrations and has to take all her meals alone. Her sense of her own strength becomes more and more evident, however. She refuses to be bullied by John any more, and hits him hard when he once again attempts to be cruel to her. When her aunt admonishes her for this, she is undaunted and argues back vehemently.

Eventually, the shadowy spectre of Mr Brocklehurst – 'a black pillar!' (p. 40) – appears. He is the warden of Lowood charity school. Mrs Reed has been making enquiries and arrangements for Jane to be sent away. This man's interrogation of Jane reveals him to be someone harsh and cruel who is guided by religious fervour. To Jane's childish eyes he reminds her of the wolf in the fairy story 'Little Red Riding Hood': 'what a great nose! and what a mouth! and what large prominent teeth!' (p. 41). Jane's description of Brocklehurst shows her a good judge of character. The childish reference to Little Red Riding Hood shows that Jane has instinctively made Brocklehurst a figure of both threat and mockery. He is diminished in our eyes by this reaction from her.

EXAMINER'S SECRET
You will gain more credit if you show you have some understanding of the novel in its historical context.

When he leaves, Jane and Mrs Reed have their final terrible encounter. Jane's emotional but honest account of her treatment shocks and undermines her aunt's authority. The power balance has finally shifted because Jane presents the truth fairly and honestly. She tells her aunt, 'I am not deceitful: if I were, I should say I loved *you*; but I declare I do not love you' (p. 45). Jane's character upholds the value of truth in all things. This idea is to become a driving theme in the novel.

Jane's need for and belief in love is highlighted by her behaviour towards the little doll she cherishes, despite its shortcomings. It is a reflection of herself: small, shoddy in appearance, almost pitiful, but still worth attention and care.

> ### Jane is growing
>
> As this phase of the novel draws to its conclusion there is a strong sense of Jane's developing integrity. Her opinions are firmer and more readily expressed, and people listen to them. Bessie's need for reassurance from Jane highlights this shift in relationship clearly.

WHO SAYS ...?

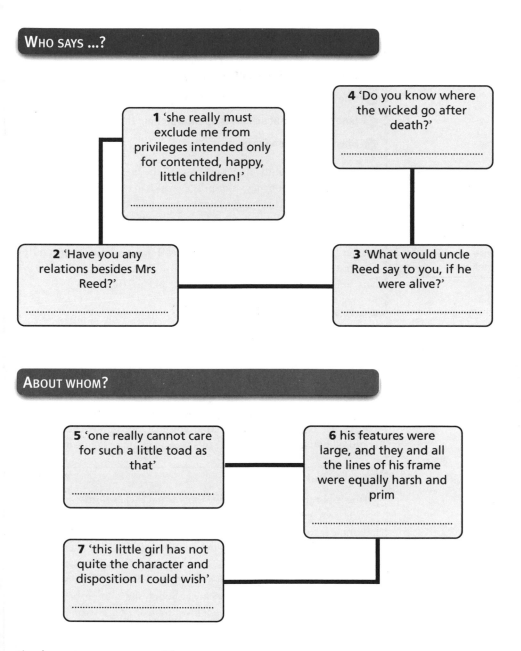

1 'she really must exclude me from privileges intended only for contented, happy, little children!'

....

4 'Do you know where the wicked go after death?'

....

2 'Have you any relations besides Mrs Reed?'

....

3 'What would uncle Reed say to you, if he were alive?'

....

ABOUT WHOM?

5 'one really cannot care for such a little toad as that'

....

6 his features were large, and they and all the lines of his frame were equally harsh and prim

....

7 'this little girl has not quite the character and disposition I could wish'

....

Check your answers on p. 97.

CHAPTER 5 – Off to school

❶ Jane travels to Lowood School alone.

❷ She arrives and meets Miss Temple.

❸ Jane's first day at school is spent watching the proceedings.

❹ She meets Helen Burns.

CHECKPOINT 2

Why might the writer give particular emphasis to Jane's sense of loneliness?

The second phase of the novel opens with the first of Jane's solitary journeys. Solitary journeys signpost every change in Jane's life. Look out for other similar journeys later in the novel. Consider how sympathy for Jane is created by drawing attention to her isolation. She travels to Lowood School alone and friendless. When she arrives she has her first meeting with the lovely Miss Temple whom she instantly recognises as someone to admire and trust. Jane comments that the lady 'impressed me with her voice, look, and air' (p. 53).

Her first day at Lowood is spent in observation – one of Jane's most familiar occupations. What she observes troubles her in part: she sees the harsh treatment of the girls, the bad food – 'The porridge is burnt again!' (p. 55) – the regimented systems. However, she does not appear afraid or daunted by any of this.

Her first meeting with the remarkable Helen Burns takes place; again, Jane clearly recognises another kindred spirit. She is, however, confused by Helen's acceptance of a seemingly unjust punishment.

First friends

Jane is instantly drawn to Miss Temple and Helen Burns, and in their own ways both have profound effects on her life. Miss Temple is to become a role model for Jane, upholding the values of strength, observance of duty and above all truth to oneself which Jane recognises in herself.

Helen, interestingly, troubles Jane although she admires her intensely. She immediately recognises someone with strong opinions and personal integrity, and is confused by the seeming acquiescence to orders and duty even when misplaced.

CHAPTER 6 – A new girl at Lowood

① **Jane becomes friends with Helen Burns.**

② **Helen's ideas sometimes trouble Jane.**

This chapter reinforces the cruelty of the regime at Lowood, again strengthened by the depiction of harsh weather conditions. The girls are given very little to eat, work long hours, have little discourse with each other and suffer extremely cold temperatures.

Jane makes more headway with her relationship with Helen Burns, questioning her closely about her beliefs. It becomes apparent that Helen will bear with fortitude any cruelty and punishment without complaint. Jane struggles with this idea, believing that one should stand up to oppression and undeserved cruelty – 'When we are struck at without a reason, we should strike back again very hard' (p. 68). Helen presents her with an alternative point of view, driven by the Christian conviction that one should bear any amount of suffering in this world in order to benefit in the afterlife, and 'Love your enemies' (p. 69). She accepts all the criticism and anger of her teachers, believing that they are right to correct and punish her for what seem to Jane to be petty and irrelevant misdemeanours.

Jane's constant questioning of Helen marks her as someone very interested in life and her place in it. She is a strong character who will not merely accept things as they are but wishes to explore and understand them. Her analytical nature is very well developed in one so young, and demonstrates her independence of mind.

Although intrigued and fascinated by Helen, and obviously very much in awe of her, she still does not blindly accept Helen's way of perceiving the world. Her innate sense of self allows her to construct her own opinions rather than slavishly adhering to those of others.

> **CHECKPOINT 3**
>
> What part does the description of the weather play in our understanding of the chapter?

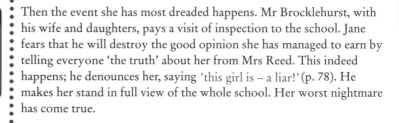

CHAPTER 7 – 'This girl is – a liar!'

1 Jane tries to settle in at Lowood.

2 Mr Brocklehurst and his family visit the school.

3 He denounces Jane as a liar.

Jane spends the next three months trying to fit into the Lowood regime, however critical she is of it. Far from being self-pitying, she stands up with determination to the cold and the long hours, and strives to work hard and achieve success. The good opinion of her teachers and fellow pupils is very important to her, and she begins to earn this with her quick mind and strenuous attempts to learn.

Then the event she has most dreaded happens. Mr Brocklehurst, with his wife and daughters, pays a visit of inspection to the school. Jane fears that he will destroy the good opinion she has managed to earn by telling everyone 'the truth' about her from Mrs Reed. This indeed happens; he denounces her, saying 'this girl is – a liar!' (p. 78). He makes her stand in full view of the whole school. Her worst nightmare has come true.

CHECKPOINT 4

What is **ironic** about the timing of Brocklehurst's wife and daughters' visit?

? DID YOU KNOW?

The depiction of the regimentation of Lowood and the tyrannical nature of Mr Brocklehurst are drawn directly from the author's experiences at boarding school.

Jane assumes that Mr Brocklehurst, as the figurehead of the school, is respected and admired by all. Reading between the lines, however, his hypocrisy is clearly apparent. His wife and daughters are dressed in the finest clothes and jewels although he believes that the way to a pure soul is to punish the body: note how he complains that a girl's naturally curly hair will lead to vanity – 'that girl's hair must be cut off' (p. 75).

When he admonishes Miss Temple for allowing the children a simple meal because their breakfast had been ruined, we see in her manner an underlying disrespect for his severity. This is another indication that Mr Brocklehurst does not in fact command the respect which Jane assumes he merits.

? **DID YOU KNOW?**
Charlotte Brontë attended a boarding school, which was founded upon staunch religious principles and was harsh and austere.

CHAPTER 8 – Jane's reputation is restored

1 **Helen Burns comforts Jane.**

2 **Helen and Jane have tea with Miss Temple.**

3 **Miss Temple promises to write to Mr Lloyd.**

4 **Jane's story is validated.**

Lost in isolation and despair, Jane is found by Helen Burns who offers her comfort by telling her that Mr Brocklehurst is not admired, respected or even liked by the school – therefore no one actually believes the accusations levelled against Jane.

Helen and Jane have conflicting views on the importance of the opinions of others. Whilst Jane prizes public approval above all things, Helen feels that personal integrity is more important. This conflict is eventually resolved in the adult Jane, who listens to herself first but still needs the love and respect of those she admires.

Miss Temple seeks the girls and invites them to tea in her room. She questions Jane closely about her time at Gateshead, and believes her account of the cruelty she suffered there. However, she promises to write to Mr Lloyd to have Jane's story corroborated. Jane listens

CHECKPOINT 5

What is interesting about the conversation over tea in the staff room?

enraptured to Miss Temple and Helen's intellectual discussion, observing and appreciating a real warmth and affinity between the two women.

A shadow is cast over the evening by a growing awareness that Helen is ill, and that Miss Temple is clearly extremely concerned about her. Reading as observers we are once again able to interpret in a way that Jane cannot. There is a sense of foreboding in Miss Temple's manner towards Helen: 'it was Helen her eye followed to the door; it was for her she a second time breathed a sad sigh; for her she wiped a tear from her cheek' (p. 86).

The reply from the apothecary indeed validates Jane's story, and in public Miss Temple addresses the school 'to pronounce her completely cleared from every imputation' (p. 86). This is a relief to Jane, and pleases her teachers and peers.

CHAPTER 9 – Helen Burns dies

1 Jane settles down at Lowood.

2 There is an outbreak of typhus at the school.

3 Helen has consumption.

4 Helen dies.

The better weather reflects Jane's altered state of mind. The year drifts into a warm spring and the mood looks set to alter. However, the warmth and damp bring a severe outburst of typhus fever to Lowood; the whole school becomes a hospital as more and more girls sicken and die from the extremely infectious fever.

Jane happily escapes from the illness; Helen, however, has developed consumption and is near to death. This she faces with the same undaunted spirit; her strength gives Jane courage and when she dies, Jane is at her side.

DID YOU KNOW?
The tender portrait of the suffering Helen Burns is thought to be a reminiscence of Brontë's, eldest sister, Maria, who died from consumption, as tuberculosis was then called.

Helen's death

Helen's death, an extremely moving part of the story, is described in a pragmatic, unemotional manner. No comment is made regarding Jane's feelings; a short passage describes the place where Helen is laid to rest and the simple inscription on her headstone, one assumes by Jane herself, fifteen years later. By not wallowing in the emotional intensity, the loss of Helen is made all the more poignant: as if no words are necessary or appropriate to honour her memory and the manner of her death. The reader is left with the **image** of the two girls clinging to each other for support and warmth. The two girls are found the next morning – 'I was asleep, and Helen was – dead' (p. 96). The scene is tender and lovely on its own, needing no lengthy emotional outpourings to reinforce it.

DID YOU KNOW?

Like Jane Eyre, Charlotte Brontë taught at a school.

CHAPTER 10 – Eight years at Lowood

❶ Lowood school is taken over by kinder people.

❷ Jane continues as pupil, then teacher at the school.

❸ Miss Temple leaves.

❹ Jane secures a job as a governess.

❺ Bessie comes to visit Jane.

The devastating effects of the typhus epidemic cause public notice to be brought to Lowood. Shocked by the harsh conditions there, the school is taken over by kinder minds.

Jane skims over the next eight years, six as a pupil and two as a teacher, mentioning her success and happiness at the school. Note how Jane's independence begins to develop as she grows older. The summary ends with the marriage and departure of her role model Miss Temple. This event causes her to become restless, and she advertises for a situation as governess. Her first knowledge of Thornfield comes in a letter from Mrs Fairfax, the housekeeper there, offering her a position. Jane recognises, 'A phase of my life was closing' (p. 104).

Bessie the servant from Gateshead, comes to visit her, telling her that her uncle came to the house some seven years before to look for her. He was on his way to the island of 'Madeira' (p. 107) and could not stay long enough to seek her out. The hint of other relations who may be beneficial is not dwelt upon by Jane, although to the careful reader this is a significant piece of information. Jane also hears that the Reeds' situation is not a happy one: news which surprises neither her nor the reader.

It is interesting to see Jane's desire for good opinion: in spite of impressing Bessie mightily with her accomplishments, she is still hurt by the notion that she is not physically appealing. Note how Jane is on a quest for happiness and fulfilment, no matter how much she denies this to herself.

GLOSSARY

Madeira an island off the coast of North Africa

Now take a break!

WHO SAYS ...?

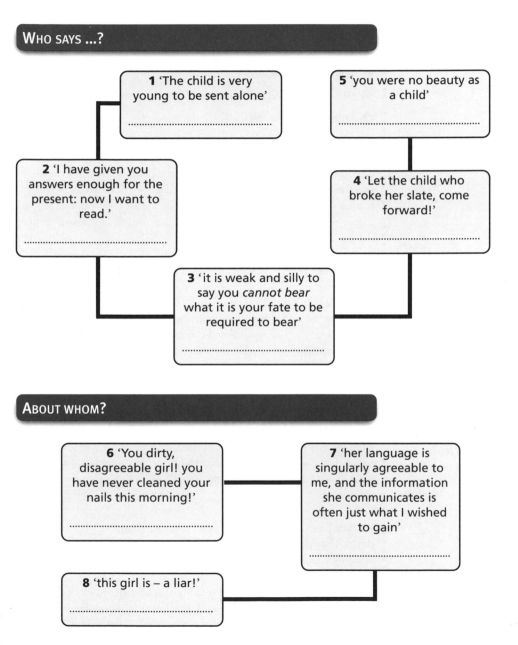

1 'The child is very young to be sent alone'

....

5 'you were no beauty as a child'

....

2 'I have given you answers enough for the present: now I want to read.'

....

4 'Let the child who broke her slate, come forward!'

....

3 'it is weak and silly to say you *cannot bear* what it is your fate to be required to bear'

....

ABOUT WHOM?

6 'You dirty, disagreeable girl! you have never cleaned your nails this morning!'

....

7 'her language is singularly agreeable to me, and the information she communicates is often just what I wished to gain'

....

8 'this girl is – a liar!'

....

Check your answers on p. 97.

Chapter 11 – Next stop, Thornfield Hall

1 Jane travels to Millcote.

2 She is welcomed at Thornfield.

3 Jane meets her pupil, Adèle.

4 Jane hears strange noises from high in the house.

The third phase of Jane's life opens with another solitary journey – this time to Millcote, the nearest town to Thornfield. Whilst waiting for her ride to the house she reflects upon her situation and muses that whilst on one level to be alone is terrifying, there is also a thrill of the unknown about it.

The fact that this is a distinct new phase of Jane's story is signalled in the opening lines: 'A new chapter in a novel is something like a new scene in a play' (p. 108). The manner of narration is also different: note how the reader is drawn far more into Jane's thoughts. Her internal workings of mind now become the focus of the story as she reaches maturity and is able to reflect more articulately on her own situation, rather than leaving readers to draw their own conclusions. Look at the way Jane reasons with herself whenever she is afraid or unsure.

DID YOU KNOW?

Charlotte Brontë taught as a governess in private households.

Jane's arrival at Thornfield is a pleasant one. She is greeted by the friendly Mrs Fairfax whom she still assumes to be the owner. She is astonished the following morning to learn that this lady is only the housekeeper and that Thornfield actually belongs to the elusive Mr Rochester.

As ever, Jane is strongly influenced by her surroundings: her first full day at Thornfield opens with a survey of the pleasant aspect from her window which cheers her immensely and hints at a better life to come.

She meets her pupil: the little French girl Adèle, Mr Rochester's ward. Note that Jane recognises Adèle's faults but does not judge her for them. In her customary manner she asks many questions of Mrs Fairfax and so begins to get the measure of Thornfield Hall. The chapter ends with strange noises from a room on a distant floor of the house, and the first mention of the mysterious name Grace Poole.

Jane's physical appearance is referred to in this chapter: 'I felt it a misfortune that I was so little, so pale, and had features so irregular and so marked' (p. 114). She examines her wish that she were more physically appealing, recognising this desire for what it is and dealing with it pragmatically.

CHAPTER 12 – Jane meets Mr Rochester

1 **Three months pass peacefully at Thornfield.**

2 **Jane meets Mr Rochester for the first time.**

The first three months of Jane's new situation pass peacefully enough. She is reasonably contented with her lot, although she is aware of her restless spirit and quest for happiness. Her companions please her, and there is a clarity and honesty in her reaction to them, as in her dispassionate response to Adèle.

> **CHECKPOINT 6**
>
> What is surprising in Jane's response to Adèle?

CHECK THE FILM

Franco Zeffirelli's film adaptation of *Jane Eyre* (1996) stars William Hurt and Charlotte Gainsbourg. It pays close attention to the importance of setting in the story.

The first meeting

This chapter contains the first, dramatic, meeting with Mr Rochester. She encounters him when he falls from his horse and she is obliged to give him assistance. Her first impression of his face is that 'He had a dark face, with stern features and a heavy brow' (p. 129). Still unaware of who he is, she is amazed on returning home to discover that the gentleman she assisted in the road is in fact her employer.

Jane's future relationship with Rochester is most clearly set out in their first meeting. Although penniless, demure and socially dependent, she is not afraid of this rather gruff-looking man, but approaches him confidently to offer her help. She gives him physical assistance and support, which is a benchmark for their unusual relationship throughout. In spite of her apparent inferiority she maintains a strength and power in relation to him, a refusal to be dominated.

Rochester's dog Pilot she describes as a 'Gytrash' (p. 178), or spirit dog. Remember her experience in the red-room of Chapter 3, when one of her visions in the fit was something with 'A great black dog behind him' (Ch. 3, p. 27). Maybe the child Jane had a premonition, a hint that this event was to begin the most remarkable aspect of her life?

CHAPTER 13 – Rochester grills the governess

1 Mr Rochester sends for Adèle and Jane.

2 Mr Rochester questions Jane closely.

3 Mrs Fairfax reveals that there were troubles in the Rochester family.

That evening Mr Rochester sends for Adèle and Jane. Adèle has been in a flurry of excitement all day, desperate for the opportunity to show off to her guardian. When the interview finally takes place, Jane feels instantly comfortable with Mr Rochester's abrupt manner and gruff composure. He questions her closely, refusing to flatter her although clearly impressed with her painting skills especially.

Jane is not intimidated by Rochester although he is clearly a rude and abrupt man. Her opinions of him are honest and forthright; she appears to take the measure of him instantly. The hint of his being dissatisfied and gloomy is reinforced by his manner towards Adèle, which is certainly lacking warmth.

The description of Jane's paintings gives a very interesting insight into her character. All three present a dreamy and passionate side to Jane which must intrigue Rochester when faced with the demure and acquiescent young governess before him.

Jane discovers from Mrs Fairfax that there were some Rochester 'Family troubles' (p. 145), and that he has to bear some kind of unhappiness, which partly explains why he seldom returns to Thornfield.

CHECKPOINT 7
How is Jane's interest in Rochester revealed?

CHAPTER 14 – Jane and Rochester spar

❶ Many visitors come to Thornfield.

❷ Rochester gives Adèle a box of gifts.

❸ Rochester and Jane have a long conversation.

Now that Mr Rochester has again become resident and master of Thornfield, the house is busy with visitors. Jane sees him infrequently, and can never predict his manner towards her when they do chance to meet on a corridor or pathway.

One evening he again sends for her and Adèle; the child is given a large box of gifts from Rochester's travels, and while she examines them in delight Jane and Rochester have their longest, most interesting conversation to date. It is interesting to see how neither Jane nor Rochester is lost for words in their conversation. Rochester is frank and honest with Jane, as she is with him, and a large part of their **dialogue** investigates the conventions of relationship between master and 'paid subordinate'.

The powerful communication between Rochester and Jane highlights the equality of mind they share, regardless of their positions in society. Jane is eloquent and articulate with him, and certainly not afraid to be honest: 'do you think me handsome?' – 'No, sir' (p. 149). He is refreshed and fascinated by her attitude of mind and refusal to be dominated.

Underneath the occasionally flippant tone and wordplay, they are examining each other closely. He is intrigued by her and the effect she has on him; her clarity enables him to be honest about himself.

CHAPTER 15 – Jane saves Rochester from a fire

1 **Jane learns about Adèle's background.**

2 **Strange noises disturb Jane in the night.**

3 **She discovers Rochester's bed is on fire.**

4 **She wakes him, and puts out the flames.**

 DID YOU KNOW?
To publish as a woman in the nineteenth century was extremely difficult; so Charlotte Brontë published *Jane Eyre* under the pseudonym of Currer Bell.

This chapter uncovers the mystery surrounding Adèle's place at Thornfield. She is 'the daughter of a French opera-dancer' (p. 160), one-time mistress of Mr Rochester. This women, Céline Varens, treated Rochester badly and was only really interested in his money. When the child came along he undertook her care, but does not believe she is his daughter. His motivation for looking after her is to purge some sin by committing a charitable deed, nothing more.

Jane does not judge Rochester for his past life, although its 'worldliness' must be a shock. Rather, she is fascinated by his attitude towards his past deeds and also the impetus which apparently drives him to bare his soul to her. This is where the reader is in a better position to judge the situation than Jane; it is clear to us that Rochester is growing to care for Jane but her natural innocence and reticence does not allow her to see this.

Her attitude to his story shows her natural integrity and independence of mind. Instead of being condemnatory, she accepts that he has made mistakes and is more interested in his desire to change and reform.

In bed that night thinking about Rochester's attitude towards her, Jane is disturbed by strange noises, and a 'demoniac laugh' (p. 168) outside her door. Investigating this, she discovers that Rochester's bed 'curtains' (p. 168) are on fire and that he is nearly unconscious from smoke inhalation. She stirs and wakes him, managing to quench the fire and save his life. His gratitude towards her has an unwarranted warmth about it, and this section of the novel ends with her presentiment of his growing affection towards her.

A worldly man

The original audience may have been more condemnatory of Mr Rochester's past behaviour than an audience of the twenty-first century. However, it is vital for the depiction of Jane's truly Christian character that she overlook the worldly mistakes of a worldly man; loving him in spite of his male humanity rather than refusing to acknowledge it.

GLOSSARY

curtains four-poster beds would have curtains around them

CHAPTER 16 – Jane tries to curb her feelings

1 Following the fire, Jane is agitated.

2 She questions Grace Poole.

3 Rochester has left to visit friends.

4 Mrs Fairfax tells Jane about the beautiful Blanche Ingram.

5 Jane paints two portraits.

Jane passes the morning after the fire in a whirl of agitation. In spite of her pragmatic and sensible nature she is convinced that what she saw and heard in Rochester's tone and eyes was love. In turn, we see in this chapter that Jane is beginning to become more and more fascinated by Rochester.

The day passes unremarkably. Jane has the opportunity to question Grace Poole regarding the events of the night before and is staggered by the woman's apparent composure and hypocrisy, believing as she does that Grace is the source of the strange noises and the cause of the fire. She entertains momentary suspicions regarding Grace's relationship to Rochester which she almost immediately dismisses as ridiculous.

CHECKPOINT 8

What evidence is there that Jane is beginning to fall in love with Rochester?

When she learns that Rochester has left to visit friends, she is perturbed. Mrs Fairfax tells her of the beautiful Blanche Ingram who will be one of the party. It becomes instantly clear to Jane that her own suspicions regarding Rochester's feelings towards her are nothing more than childish fancy. She seeks to destroy her feelings by painting two portraits: an imaginary one of Blanche which she makes as exquisite as possible, and a dowdy one of herself, entitled 'Portrait of a Governess, disconnected, poor, and, plain' (p. 183).

Jane's strength of character is keenly visible here. Although her growing love for Rochester is palpable to the reader, Jane refuses to fuel these feelings, and instead forces herself to stare reality in the face by painting the miniatures.

Rochester's sudden departure is difficult to interpret as we are not privy to his inner workings of mind; thus we have to think beyond

Jane's interpretation of events and judge for ourselves why he may have left Thornfield – and her – so suddenly.

CHAPTER 17 – The lovely Miss Ingram?

① **Rochester is coming back to Thornfield.**

② **The house is prepared.**

③ **Jane overhears a conversation about Grace Poole.**

④ **The party of people arrive.**

⑤ **Jane studies Blanche and Rochester closely.**

After two weeks of silence, a letter announces the imminent return of Rochester with a large party of guests. The whole house is made ready, and for three days there is a flurry of activity. Jane anxiously awaits the sight of Rochester and Blanche Ingram.

The mystery surrounding Grace Poole deepens as Jane overhears a whispered conversation between two maids regarding Grace's large salary and the difficult nature of her job. She discovers that she is being deliberately kept in the dark, but soon forgets to think of this as thoughts of Rochester take over.

 DID YOU KNOW?
With all literature, a character's response to those around them is often a good indicator of their own personality.

DID YOU KNOW?

Charlotte Brontë started writing *Jane Eyre* while she was caring for her father who had undergone an eye operation.

The evening after the arrival of the party, Mr Rochester sends word for Adèle and Jane to come downstairs after dinner. Jane is extremely reluctant but Rochester is adamant. Whilst the guests entertain themselves, Jane is able to remain unobserved and studies Blanche and Rochester closely, interpreting the relationship between them as one of courtship. Seeing an opportunity to escape, she slips away but is intercepted in the hallway by Rochester and is unable to disguise her emotional distress.

Again the telltale signs of Rochester's feelings for Jane are clearly visible to the reader. The considerate nature of his tone towards her, his demand that she be present with the party every evening, his sudden pause: 'Goodnight, my –' (p. 205) all clearly denote the behaviour of a man in love.

In contrast, note the ribaldry and flirtatious tone adopted in the conversation between him and Blanche Ingram: although entertaining and articulate, there is a lack of depth and sincerity already visible in their discourse with each other.

CHAPTER 18 – Charades, and a stranger

① Jane continues to observe Blanche and Rochester.

② Her love for Rochester deepens.

③ Jane realises Blanche is harsh and cold.

④ Mr Mason arrives at Thornfield.

⑤ A beggar woman arrives to tell the ladies' fortunes.

As the days progress, Jane has ample opportunity to observe and study the relationship between Blanche and Rochester. Jane's description of Blanche's behaviour is particularly unflattering. Her cruel nature is shown in her manner towards Adèle, and her haughty attitude to Jane. Jane's love for Rochester deepens constantly, as does her horror at the dawning realisation that Blanche, in spite of being beautiful, accomplished and ladylike, is harsh and cold. When she realises that Rochester himself knows this and does not love her, she is devastated. She could have accepted the situation if there was genuine love between them, but is tormented at the idea that he will marry for 'family, perhaps political reasons; because her rank and connexions suited him' (p. 211).

One gloomy evening, after Rochester has been away all day on business, first a Mr Mason arrives at Thornfield, then a beggar woman arrives desiring to tell the fortunes of all the young ladies. The guests gladly seize on this opportunity of distraction; Blanche, however, is clearly very disturbed by what she is told. The fortune-teller – described by a servant as 'A shockingly ugly old creature' (p. 217) – refuses to leave without an audience with Jane.

Jane's control and calm in the face of a visit to the gypsy directly contrasts with the hysterical shrieks of some of the ladies, highlighting her dignity and personal integrity.

Here we fully appreciate the magnitude of Jane's feelings for Rochester; the selflessness of the love she feels for him. It never enters her head to include herself in any ideas of his future happiness, but she sincerely wants him to make a marriage of love for his own sake.

> **CHECKPOINT 9**
>
> How is Jane's goodness revealed in her response to Blanche's behaviour?

CHAPTER 19 – Jane and the gypsy

1 **Jane goes in to see the gypsy.**

2 **She realises it is Rochester in disguise.**

3 **He is shocked to hear that Mr Mason has arrived.**

4 **Rochester escorts Mr Mason to a guest room.**

Jane has her interview with the 'gypsy' who attempts to draw her out and get her to give her opinions of the party, especially Rochester and Miss Ingram. The dialogue between them grows stranger and stranger, until finally Jane realises who the gypsy is and 'Mr Rochester stepped out of his disguise' (p. 228).

EXAMINER'S SECRET

A feature of 'A'-grade writing on literature is the ability to see two possibilities of interpretations and to support a preference for one of them.

The lovely initial banter between the 'gypsy' and Jane is far superior to similar ironic conversations between Rochester and Blanche. Jane is clearly equal to Rochester in intellect, sense and feeling if not social status or age.

The fact that Jane has suspicions that the woman is Rochester in disguise is testament to how well she has studied him; she knows him much better than his 'fiancée'. At the same time, Rochester has been observing Jane as keenly as she observed him: his comments display accurate and sensitive judgements of her personality and feelings.

Rochester reacts with stunned shock to the news that a Mr Mason from Jamaica has arrived at Thornfield; indeed, Jane has never seen him look so troubled, almost afraid. She appears a little bemused by his behaviour but has no time to reflect upon it. The evening closes amicably enough, with Rochester apparently in jovial conversation with Mason as he escorts him to a guest room for the night.

A tricky situation?

Rochester's decision to play such a trick certainly displays a keen desire to investigate Jane's true feelings for him.

CHAPTER 20 – A scream, an attack, a walk

1 A cry disturbs the household.

2 Rochester calls on Jane for help.

3 She looks after Mr Mason, who has been attacked by Mrs Poole.

4 Rochester leaves, returning with a doctor.

5 Jane and Rochester walk in the gardens.

The household is disturbed in the night by a terrible cry, 'a savage, a sharp, a shrilly sound' (p. 232). Although Rochester manages to soothe everyone by claiming the noise is nothing more than a servant's nightmare, Jane is not convinced. She is right in her suspicions; Rochester calls her to his aid once again, this time to tend to Mr Mason, who has been viciously attacked, presumably by the strange Mrs Poole. Jane's courage is severely called upon as she has to stay by Mason for two hours in the dark whilst Rochester goes for a doctor. He has been forbidden to speak to her on any account.

Once again Jane is shown to be resourceful and courageous; the other ladies were practically hysterical at Mason's first shriek, but Jane copes with these terrible events with fortitude.

The circumstances into which Jane is placed here would thrill and delight the nineteenth-century readers. The Gothic setting with the invalid, the blood, the dark, the strange noises and mysterious threatening presence, all combine to create a sense of mystery and to highlight Jane's innocence and vulnerability.

Eventually Rochester returns with the doctor, and Mason is carried away. Jane and her employer walk in the gardens, and once again there is a warmth and tenderness in his manner towards her. However, he also asks whether she would be there to keep him company on the evening before his wedding to Miss Ingram; there is sarcasm and harshness in his tone when he mentions that name and subject.

The strength of Rochester's feelings for her are even more palpable in this chapter, but Jane seems oblivious to them. When he speaks of the

> **CHECKPOINT 10**
>
> What do we learn about Jane from her reaction to the terrible cry in the night?

'good and bright qualities … all fresh, healthy, without soil and without taint' (p. 245), it is clearly Jane he refers to.

CHAPTER 21 – Return to Aunt Reed

① Jane's aunt Reed is dying.

② Jane takes leave of Rochester and returns to Gateshead.

③ Mrs Reed tells Jane about her uncle.

The chapter opens with her musing on the workings of fate, a strong idea in the novel. Note how Jane's growing strength of character and desire to do the right thing are reinforced here.

CHECK THE BOOK

The Wide Sargasso Sea (1966) by Jean Rhys is the story of Bertha Rochester, told partly from her point of view and partly from the young Rochester's. It gives a very interesting slant on the story of *Jane Eyre*.

The recurrent dream of the baby is perhaps a personification of the innocence and vulnerability of Jane herself; she has to be her own support and carer because she is alone in the world.

The next day Jane is sent for by her aunt Reed, who is near to death. Her son John has led a 'very wild' (p. 249) and irresponsible life, almost bringing his mother to financial ruin. News of his death has brought on a stroke, but she cannot rest until she has spoken to her niece.

After taking leave of Rochester and being entreated with a promise to return as soon as possible, Jane hastens away. Note the nature of the conversation: it is resonant with implied meaning, charged with emotion underneath the surface banter.

At Gateshead Jane finds her cousins Eliza and Georgiana, both unlikeable and selfish women in their way, waiting impatiently for their mother's death so that they can resume their lives. It comes as no surprise that the Reeds have not had successful lives: the implicit message being that selfishness and cruelty can only lead to misery. Jane is in the enviable position of being able to rise above them all and view them dispassionately because she recognises that she no longer needs or respects them. Mrs Reed, as cold and austere towards Jane as ever, tells her that she received a request some three years before from Jane's uncle that she be sent to join him in Madeira. Mrs Reed hated Jane so much that she told him 'Jane Eyre was dead' (p. 268). Although she still hates Jane, some pricking of the conscience has forced her to clear her mind of this action before she can die. Jane has a huge capacity for forgiveness and we will see this again later in the novel.

Once again, Jane's reaction to traumatic news is strange; she could have been living a very different life if only her aunt had acted more kindly but, as she would never have met Rochester in this case, any regret seems irrelevant.

CHAPTER 22 – Home to Thornfield

1 **Jane returns to Thornfield.**

2 **She prepares herself for her pain when Rochester marries.**

3 **Rochester is delighted to see her.**

4 **Jane begins to hope he and Blanche will not marry.**

Jane returns to Thornfield: another journey, this one a mixture of anticipation and fear for the future. The prospect of seeking a further job does not distress her; in fact she refuses to think that far ahead. She is too intent upon preparing herself for the pain she will feel when Rochester marries.

Jane finally acknowledges her deep love for Rochester. She recognises that this much self-denial is futile and all her efforts to keep a check on her feelings will still not protect her from the pain of losing him.

The powerful force of her feelings for Rochester is intensified by the shift into present tense as she approaches Thornfield (pp. 274–5). The effect of this technique is to remove the distance of time from Jane's narration, and make the event appear much more immediate.

> **CHECKPOINT 11**
>
> What evidence do we have of Jane's self-control?

EXAMINER'S SECRET

Plan your answers then you won't repeat yourself.

Rochester is delighted to see her: his highly animated language and tone show this clearly. She is welcomed by Mrs Fairfax and Adèle, and two weeks pass tranquilly with no sign of any wedding preparations. Jane begins to hope and suspect that the marriage is not, in fact, going to take place.

CHAPTER 23 – A proposal of marriage

❶ Jane takes an evening walk in the garden.

❷ She tries to avoid Rochester.

❸ Rochester persuades her to walk with him.

❹ He asks Jane to marry him.

❺ She accepts with great joy.

Taking a walk in the garden on a beautiful midsummer's evening, Jane becomes aware of Rochester's presence and tries to avoid him, feeling uncomfortable in his company. He has been watching her and is now apparently following her, and persuades her to walk with him in the orchard.

It is in this idyllic setting that the final truth of his feelings becomes clear; he denies the existence of any engagement to Miss Ingram and pleads instead for Jane's hand in marriage. At first aghast, she is transported into pure joy when she realises that he is being sincere and genuinely loves her.

Setting is again very important to this moment. Think why the author chooses a lovely night for the proposal. Note again the pathetic fallacy in the weather conditions, echoing and reinforcing Jane's happiness.

The sudden break in the weather resulting in the storm which splits the horse chestnut tree into two is a clear omen, signifying that this impending union is not right.

EXAMINER'S SECRET

Keep a note of the weather for important scenes. This will help you with questions about both setting and imagery.

Rochester's manner and language also hint towards all not being well: the 'savagery' with which he holds to Jane and his defiance of 'the world's judgment' (p. 287) present a cause for concern. 'He set his teeth' (p. 284) in determination. However, Jane is oblivious to all this, so enraptured is she by this change in her fortunes.

It is reasonable to be slightly concerned by the way Rochester plays his game with Jane right up to the last minute: torturing her with the idea of his marriage to another. One interpretation of his behaviour is that he is forcing her into a confession of her real feelings in order to be sure that his suspicions are correct.

All is not well

The sheer desperation evident in Rochester's blinkered, relentless pursual of Jane makes this scene ominous and vaguely unsettling. In spite of its containing one of the most moving and eloquent proposals in literature, the reader is left with a sense of ominous foreboding.

CHAPTER 24 – Wedding plans

❶ Jane is anxious to see Rochester.

❷ Mrs Fairfax is cool towards her.

❸ Rochester takes Jane shopping.

❹ Jane avoids sentimental behaviour in the month before the wedding.

❺ Jane writes to her uncle.

The following morning Jane is anxious to see Rochester to make sure she has not dreamed the wonderful events of the previous evening. Mrs Fairfax is cool towards her, having witnessed an embrace between them, and Jane requests that she explain the truth to her immediately. Her caution is upsetting to Jane although Mrs Fairfax's worries are justified and reasonable, with a tinge of ironic warning: 'I do fear there will be something found to be different to what either you or I expect' (p. 297).

CHECKPOINT 12

How does this chapter illustrate Jane's strength of character?

Rochester takes Jane shopping, but she is uncomfortable with his attempts to shower her with expensive gifts. She feels that their relationship should not be transformed into a 'society match' by such trappings, and is equally uneasy with his repeated protestations of love towards her. Note how Jane stands up to Rochester in spite of being in love with him. She manages successfully to steer him away from sentimental behaviour, and the month leading up to the marriage passes with her in control of the situation.

It is not easy to interpret the reasons for Jane's behaviour here. She loves Rochester desperately and completely: 'My future husband was becoming to me my whole world; and more than the world: almost my hope of heaven' (p. 307). Yet she shies away from his desire to lavish her with affection and gifts. She perhaps feels that he should love her for herself and not attempt to invalidate the relationship between them by making it appear the same as any other in his social circle. Also, her need to be true to herself and to be independent is a powerful aspect of her personality, not to be denied even when transported by love.

She also decides to write to her uncle, feeling that some form of financial independence, however modest, would ease the discomfort she suffers due to the gap between them.

CHAPTER 25 – A ghost

1 Jane is restless.

2 She goes to meet Rochester.

3 Jane tells Rochester of her dream.

4 She also says she saw a strange woman in her room.

5 Rochester blames the incident on Grace Poole.

The day before the wedding Jane is unsettled and restless. As so often, the weather reflects her mood. Here it is overcast and stormy. Jane waits impatiently for Rochester to return home, eventually going to meet him and greeting him with unaccustomed warmth and sincerity.

Eventually she tells him that she had a very vivid dream which had a sense of omen about it. The dream again involved the idea of being burdened with a young child, and showed Jane and Rochester being separated for ever. She then tells him that on waking from this dream she discovered a strange, fearful woman with a 'savage face' (p. 317) in her room who tore her wedding veil apart before leaving the bedroom.

Rochester is evidently much shaken by this, although he gives her a reasonable explanation for the occurrence, blaming Grace Poole once again and surmising that Jane was half asleep and did not recognise her. Although not convinced, Jane tries to appear mollified, and promises to sleep in the nursery with Adèle and Sophie, rather than remain in her own room and be afraid.

Rochester evidently has another motive for keeping Jane away from her own room; he senses a real threat to her safety and wants to keep her protected. There is more going on than Jane is aware of and the appearance of this strange woman frightens Rochester disproportionately, given his explanation of the mystery.

CHECKPOINT 13

Why does Jane accept Rochester's unconvincing explanation for the vivid dream?

Again, physical events seem guided and influenced by spiritual, or even psychic features; the weather, Jane's dreams, signs and indicators are as much involved in the course of events as substantial concrete affairs.

CHAPTER 26 – An impediment!

CHECK THE BOOK

If you enjoyed *Jane Eyre*, you might like other books by Charlotte Brontë; *Shirley* (1849) and *Villette* (1853) are the most widely known.

❶ The day of the wedding has come.

❷ Jane notices two strangers enter the church.

❸ In the ceremony, a man declares that Rochester is already married.

❹ They return to the house and we see the first Mrs Rochester.

❺ Jane goes to her room.

On the day of the wedding Rochester is hurried and restless, 'grimly resolute' (p. 322). Jane notices two strangers who enter the quiet church by a side door.

When the service comes to questioning whether there is 'any lawful impediment', one of the men steps forward. He is a lawyer who declares that 'Mr Rochester has a wife now living' (p. 324). Mrs Rochester lives at Thornfield Hall and Mr Rochester is thus attempting to commit bigamy. It transpires that Jane's uncle knows Richard Mason, the brother of Mrs Rochester, and when Jane wrote to inform him of her impending marriage the alarm was raised.

Rochester leads them all to the house where we are confronted by the spectre of the first Mrs Rochester – a mad woman, closeted in an attic under the guard of Grace Poole. She violently attacks him, apparently not for the first time.

In this scene, Jane remains an observer as if she has retreated from her feelings in shock. She manages to preserve her calm in the face of all this information, only relinquishing her hold on her feelings when alone in her room. She has nothing now except her belief in God and herself.

Once the mystery is finally explained, much of the subtext of the story so far becomes clear. Jane's sense of a mystery at Thornfield, the sight of the strange woman in her room, the fearsome attack on Richard Mason, the unearthly laughs and noises are all now in context.

Rochester's behaviour is surely cause for scrutiny here. He calls upon a higher court than that of the world to judge whether he in fact was acting immorally, given his suffering since being tricked into marrying this woman for his family's financial gain. Jane does not judge him; she loves him too well and also believes in a similar kind of moral code.

CHECK THE FILM
A rather gloomy version of *Jane Eyre* (1944), starring Orson Welles and Joan Fontaine, is very dark and threatening and clearly recognises what setting adds to the story.

A hero or villain?

Recent literary criticism has leapt upon Rochester's behaviour towards his 'wife' and condemned him without reservation. However, Brontë leaves the reader to decide upon whether he should be condemned in this way or pitied for his predicament.

CHAPTER 27 – Flee temptation!

① Jane tries to imagine a solution.

② She refuses to run away with Rochester.

③ He tells her the full story about his first wife.

④ He speaks of his love.

⑤ Jane leaves the house during the night.

After a terrible period alone with her thoughts, Jane stirs and looks about for an answer. The awful solution – 'Leave Thornfield at once' (p. 335) – is so horrendous that she tries to turn from it, but it is the only possible solution. During a passionate interview with Rochester he pleads with her to run away with him, but she refuses.

CHECKPOINT 14

Why does Jane decide to leave Rochester?

He tells her the full story of his marriage to Bertha Mason. His father arranged it so that he would have a fortune of his own, the Masons being a rich family who would give a dowry of £30,000. It soon appeared that she was insane, as was her mother, and Rochester lived a terrible life with her in Jamaica before bringing her to Thornfield and shutting her away. He then ran away to Europe where he led a debauched and discontented life.

When he speaks of the effect Jane had upon him, we see the full force, beauty and sincerity of his love for her. She is almost powerless to resist this, but is resolved to 'keep the law given by God' (p. 356). Although it breaks her heart, she steals away in the night.

This bravery in the midst of total despair is quite astounding. Her sense of self is an intrinsic aspect of her nature, and never is its force more keenly felt than at the brink of temptation: '*I* care for myself. The more solitary, the more friendless, the more unsustained I am, the more I will respect myself' (p. 356). Her fundamental creed is clearly established: 'Do as I do: trust in God and yourself' (p. 355).

To a modern reader this adherence to a moral and religious code at the expense of total happiness is hard to appreciate; even some nineteenth-century readers would struggle with her dilemma. Religious beliefs and societal codes were far more influential than they appear today, and Jane was acting under the fear of disgrace and God's punishment.

She forgives Rochester completely because she understands the circumstances and because she sees how much he loves her. He is acting under the direction of an alternative moral code, not out of immorality. In spite of this understanding she cannot agree to his plan.

EXAMINER'S SECRET

In this rather melodramatic section, try to see how Jane is motivated, rather than how you might have reacted.

You decide!

One of the skills of a good writer is to allow for the reader to decide for themselves; to enable us to form our own opinion, in other words. Brontë merely presents the facts – albeit from Jane's point of view – and then steps back to allow us to decide for ourselves about the appropriateness of each character's behaviour.

Who says ...?

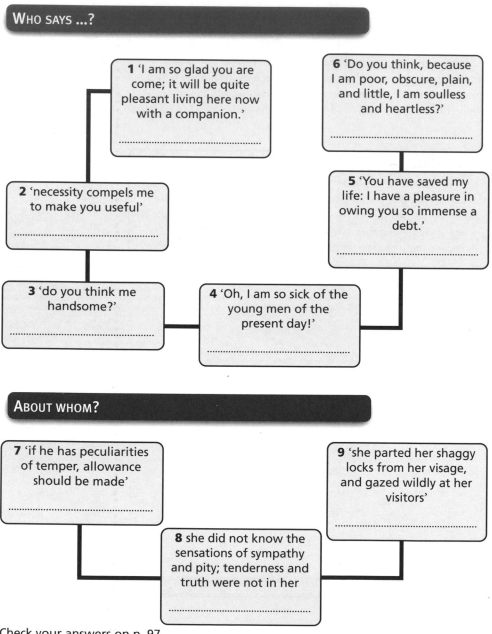

1 'I am so glad you are come; it will be quite pleasant living here now with a companion.'

....

2 'necessity compels me to make you useful'

....

3 'do you think me handsome?'

....

4 'Oh, I am so sick of the young men of the present day!'

....

6 'Do you think, because I am poor, obscure, plain, and little, I am soulless and heartless?'

....

5 'You have saved my life: I have a pleasure in owing you so immense a debt.'

....

About whom?

7 'if he has peculiarities of temper, allowance should be made'

....

8 she did not know the sensations of sympathy and pity; tenderness and truth were not in her

....

9 'she parted her shaggy locks from her visage, and gazed wildly at her visitors'

....

Check your answers on p. 97.

CHAPTER 28 – From beggar to guest

1 Jane roams the countryside looking for work.

2 She tries to beg for food.

3 After three days, she sees a candle shining in the distance.

4 She watches its inhabitants through the window.

5 The servant sends her away, but the master of the house brings her in.

Totally destitute and alone, Jane wanders the countryside in search of some means of continued existence. She looks about for work but finds nothing and no one to help her. Within a matter of hours she is reduced to begging for scraps of food. Her innate pride and delicacy is severely tested, but she still has enough sense to recognise that the needs of the body must be addressed. Several times she wishes for death, but the thought of leaving the earth with Rochester still living is unbearable to her.

The inherent **pathos** of this chapter is very powerful. Jane does not wish to dwell on sordid details, but she relates enough for the reader to feel her suffering keenly. For one so independent to be forced into

CHECKPOINT 15

Why does Charlotte Brontë have Jane walk for a long distance?

this position highlights the force of her integrity: she would rather suffer all this than be with the man she loves.

CHECKPOINT 16

What might the candle shining in a distant window represent?

After three days spent in this terrible way, she sees a candle shining feebly in the distance across a barren heath. The house she approaches is her last hope; she observes the inmates through the window and is driven by some sense of their familiarity to knock and beg for help. The servant Hannah drives her away, but the master of the house finds her on the step and hearing her call to God for help, is intrigued and brings her inside.

From a few minutes' observation she feels an empathy with the women within: 'I seemed intimate with every lineament' (p. 372). For some reason she senses a connection here: of course she is correct, and this reinforces our faith in her judgement and intuition.

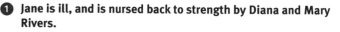

CHAPTER 29 – Recovery

❶ Jane is ill, and is nursed back to strength by Diana and Mary Rivers.

❷ Jane explains some of her past without revealing details.

❸ St John Rivers promises to help find her work.

Jane passes three days at Moor House in a state of nervous collapse, tenderly nursed by Diana and Mary Rivers. She gradually regains her strength and is soon able to sit downstairs. The initial distrust of the servant Hannah is dissipated once they have a conversation and Hannah realises that Jane is honest, decent, and well educated, certainly not the fraudster she suspected: 'You look a raight down dacent little crater' (p. 383).

Diana and Mary continue to be fascinated by Jane but their sensitivity prevents them from asking too many questions. Their brother, however, is more forthright, and Jane feels it only fair that he be given as much honest explanation as possible without alluding to Rochester and Thornfield. He appears satisfied with what she tells him and promises to do what he is able to find her honest work. St John evidently respects Jane for her honesty and integrity. He is studying her and is satisfied with what he sees.

Mary and Diana seem to recognise the same fellow-feeling in Jane as she does in them; they warm to her instantly and trust her absolutely. Their kindness and generosity is plain.

Note the attention to detail in the descriptions of the Rivers family and their home. Jane approves of the house: it is plain and functional, yet clean and warm. This is another example of her sensible value judgements which care nothing for fancy trappings and rich adornments.

CHECKPOINT 17

What does the Rivers family's lack of overt curiosity show about their character?

CHAPTER 30 – Happiness with the Rivers family

❶ Jane enjoys her time with Diana and Mary.

❷ Three weeks pass.

❸ St John asks her to be the teacher at the new local school.

❹ A letter tells of the death of the Rivers' uncle.

Jane continues to delight in the company of Diana and Mary. The three have remarkably similar tastes and attitudes, and a strong bond of affection quickly develops.

Three weeks pass, during which Jane hears nothing from St John about the promised employment.

In her customary manner she continues to observe him closely, and discovers him to be fiercely religious. His church sermons distress her because they are so fervent and smack of someone desperately searching for a way to devote his life wholeheartedly to God.

Eventually he tells her that he needs someone to set up a small school for girls in the nearby village of Moreton. She leaps at this opportunity, much to his pleasure.

CHECKPOINT 18

Why do you think Charlotte Brontë allows Jane to form a gloomy picture of St John?

Note St John's astute comments regarding Jane: 'human affections and sympathies have a most powerful hold on you' (p. 398). He is a good judge of character, as this and other observations prove.

A letter comes with news of the death of the Rivers' uncle; some family disagreement means that he has not left his fortune to them but 'bequeathed every penny to the other relation' (p. 400), who remains unnamed. The sisters have to leave home to return to their jobs as governesses, and Jane prepares to start her school.

CHECKPOINT 19

Why does Brontë have the Rivers family inherit money?

We see that the Rivers family react to life in much the same way that Jane does. They respond pragmatically to the news that they have been left without what should surely have been their legacy. Their lives would have been made much happier with even a little money, instead of which the sisters have to return to their hated professions in unfriendly households.

The observant reader will have of course picked up the link between Jane's ailing uncle John and the Rivers family's recently deceased uncle John. However, this information, like so much else of the mystery, is left in the air until such time as all the threads of the story can be bound together.

CHAPTER 31 – Schoolmistress

❶ Jane starts as mistress of the school.

❷ St John warns her against temptation.

❸ Miss Oliver arrives.

❹ Jane realises Miss Oliver and St John are in love with each other.

Jane spends her first day as mistress of the school, in 'yonder bare, humble school-room' (p. 401). When it is over she struggles with herself for feeling sad when she should be contented and happy; concern for Rochester plagues her thoughts. She does not regret her decision, however, and knows that she is in some measure being rewarded for acting correctly. Although Jane is unhappy she feels she has chosen the right path.

St John visits her and, guessing correctly at the source of her distress, warns against yielding to temptation and always instead attempting to lead a godly life. Miss Oliver, the beautiful daughter of a wealthy landowner, arrives. Jane immediately spots that St John is completely in love with this girl, who is also apparently infatuated with him. Jane's admiration for beauty has no sense of envy about it; she can value a beautiful face sincerely, but does not put as much store by physical appearance as good character.

CHECKPOINT 20

What consolations does life as a schoolmistress offer Jane?

Love and Christianity

Consider the symmetry in St John's devotion for Miss Oliver, and Jane's for Rochester. Both turn away from the fierce love they feel: both are immensely affected by it but choose not to give in to it. However, Jane's inevitable return to her love marks the essential difference between their interpretation of Christianity. Jane believes that doing God's will should not necessarily involve self-sacrifice and torment to such an extent, but to live a happy life.

CHAPTER 32 – St John steals a piece of paper

1 Jane is settling in to her new life.

2 Jane talks to St John about his love for Miss Oliver.

3 St John tears a scrap off Jane's drawing paper.

Jane settles in well to her new life, and is soon accepted by the neighbourhood. She finds much to be satisfied with, but is still tormented regularly by dreams of Rochester.

CHECKPOINT 21

Why is Miss Oliver introduced into the novel?

The deep love St John feels for Rosamund Oliver becomes more apparent, as does her affection for him. One evening as Jane is making the finishing touches to a painting of the lady, St John enters and his reaction to the lovely face prompts Jane into a frank discussion with him. She feels that if they were to marry, he could make better use of his fortune by helping those more needy by going abroad as a missionary. He acknowledges his love for the girl, but is determined to stick to his course. He argues that their marriage would not work as they are such different characters, and would tire of each other within a year.

Further exploration of St John's refusal to take the path of love and happiness reveals similarities with Jane, but not so direct as first appeared. He blindly follows the one path of missionary: his zealous religious beliefs dominating all other feeling. Where Jane turned away from love in fear of disgrace and misery, St John chooses to denounce the feeling he has for Rosamund because he has already committed himself to another road in life, whatever the personal cost. His stern nature commands him at all times, even restricting the time he allows Jane to talk of Rosamund to him: '"go on for another quarter of an hour." And he actually took out his watch and laid it upon the table to measure the time' (p. 416).

As he is leaving he notices something scribbled on a scrap of Jane's drawing paper which obviously shocks him; he quickly tears it away and leaves hurriedly.

CHAPTER 33 – A fortune and a family!

1 St John returns.

2 He tells Jane about her own past.

3 She discovers she has been left a fortune by her uncle.

4 She also learns that St John, Diana and Mary are her cousins.

The next night sees the return of St John who has struggled through a severe snowstorm to get to Jane's cottage, clearly on important business. After a period of silent contemplation he narrates to her her own history, proving that he is in full possession of the truth. Although shocked, she is far more concerned with any news of Rochester he may have, and fiercely defends St John's judgement of the former's behaviour.

When she hears that the country has been searched for her because she has been left a fortune of £20,000 by her uncle, she is staggered. When it further transpires that St John, Diana and Mary are her family – first cousins, in fact – she is delighted and immediately insists that the fortune be split four ways: it 'could never be mine in justice, though it might be in law' (p. 431).

Family is very important to Jane: remember St John's observation that 'human affections and sympathies have a most powerful hold upon you' (Ch. 30, p. 398). She is more excited by the idea that she is now part of a family, having been always a friendless orphan. The refusal to accept the full sum also highlights the aspect of her character which values love, friendship and decency above finance and its trappings.

> **CHECKPOINT 22**
>
> What is interesting about Jane's readiness to divide her fortune with the Rivers?

> **Justice**
>
> The existence of a kind of natural justice, a moral and fair system which can sometimes go against society's legal system, has echoes back to Rochester's appeal to a higher court than that of man to judge his actions. This reinforces the idea that Jane and Rochester have similar ways of viewing the world.

CHAPTER 34 – Another proposal of marriage

1. **Jane prepares Moor House for Mary and Diana's return.**

2. **A pleasant routine is established.**

3. **St John asks Jane to help him with his language studies.**

4. **Jane is unable to find out what has happened to Rochester.**

5. **St John asks Jane to marry him.**

Jane works hard to make Moor House ready for the return of Mary and Diana. The three are delighted to see each other again, and life settles down into a warm and happy routine very quickly. St John becomes more distant, however, and appears to be studying Jane much of the time. He asks her to assist him in his study of Hindustanee, a language he needs to master before he goes to India as a missionary. His hold over her becomes more and more pronounced, and she feels a claustrophobic need to please him at all times, as if he is constantly judging her.

CHECKPOINT 23

What do we notice in the way Jane responds to Mary, Diana and St John?

Several months pass. Jane tries to find out what has happened to Rochester, but meets with no success. She becomes more and more despondent as she waits in vain for news. On one occasion, when she is moved to tears, St John asks her to take a walk during which he asks her to come with him as a missionary. She agrees to this, feeling it futile to stay any longer waiting for 'some impossible change in circumstances' (p. 450) which might bring her back to the man she loves. However, St John also wants her to marry him, and this she cannot agree to, knowing that her idea of love is so different from his.

She comments on the aspect of her nature that always complies with characters stronger than her own up to the moment of 'determined revolt' (p. 446). There are echoes of the confrontations with Mrs Reed and Rochester in her interview with St John.

In spite of everything, Jane remains firm in her ideas about love. Her passionate side which values the beauty of true love is clearly displayed in her rejection of St John's offer. She rejects the idea of being 'forced to keep the fire of my nature continually low, to compel it to burn inwardly and never utter a cry, though the imprisoned flame consumed vital after vital' (p. 453): a dramatic and moving description of the horror she feels at living in a loveless marriage.

CHAPTER 35 – Jane hears Rochester's call

① **St John is cold towards Jane.**

② **She tries to improve the situation.**

③ **Jane is moved to accept his proposal.**

④ **She hears Rochester's voice calling her.**

St John retreats from Jane emotionally: although polite, he is cold and distant. She feels this deeply and continually tries to make amends, although she still refuses absolutely to be his wife. When Mary and Diana hear of his proposal they are equally determined that the idea would be terrible and that she should on no account marry him on these terms.

However, his coldness has a marked effect on her. The day before he is to leave, she is so beaten down by his refusal to be her friend that, when he asks her one last time to change her mind she is swayed into accepting. Note the similarity in Jane's position here to that of Chapter 27 when Rochester pleads with her. Again she is placed in a difficult dilemma and is tempted in spite of her better judgement. At this very moment, one charged with emotion, she hears 'a voice somewhere cry' (p. 466) – Rochester's voice is calling her desperately.

The moving poetry of this last section of the chapter is very dramatic, calculated to draw the reader into the emotion of the events to participate in the sense of climax to the story. Much has been written of the experience that Jane and Rochester share, that of 'hearing' each other over a long distance. She asks us to judge for ourselves, and one explanation could be that they share an extreme emotion at the same moment which somehow enables them to communicate with each other. To dissect this rather than accept it is to undermine the force of

EXAMINER'S SECRET
Short, snappy quotations are always the best.

GLOSSARY
vital organ

EXAMINER'S SECRET

Higher-level achievement begins at the point when you show you are aware of being marked.

this part of the **narrative**. The idea of spiritual communication reinforces the notion of a 'sympathy' between them.

Romanticism

There is no denying that Charlotte Brontë was a romantic. Living such an emotionally impoverished existence during much of her young life appears to have invested her writing with passionate outpourings which were safer in fiction than reality. However, this particular passage of the novel cannot fail to move even the most cynical reader.

Now take a break!

WHO SAYS ...?

1 'Why do I struggle to retain a valueless life?'

....

5 'I am cold: no fervour infects me'

....

2 'my heart rather warms to the poor little soul'

....

4 'I am sure you cannot long be content to pass your leisure in solitude'

....

3 'if you are a Christian, you ought not to consider poverty a crime'

....

ABOUT WHOM?

6 'You tremble and become flushed whenever Miss Oliver enters the school-room'

....

8 'you are docile, diligent, disinterested, faithful, constant, and courageous'

....

7 'She is well named the Rose of the World, indeed!'

....

Check your answers on p. 97.

CHAPTER 36 – To Thornfield again

1 Jane returns to Thornfield.

2 She finds it in ruins.

3 Following a fire, Rochester is blind and Mrs Rochester is dead.

4 Rochester now lives at Ferndean Manor.

CHECKPOINT 24

How has Jane changed as a person by this point in the novel?

Bent on a purpose which directs her every move, Jane prepares to return to Thornfield to ascertain once and for all what has happened to Rochester. She takes another journey in the same coach which carried her to Marsh End a year before. After making some enquiries, she walks to Thornfield and is shocked and dismayed to find it a 'blackened ruin' (p. 472).

Hurrying back to the inn, she hears from the owner that Mrs Rochester had started a fire in Jane's bed before throwing herself from the battlements. Rochester, who had become distraught after Jane's disappearance, saves the servants and tries to help his wife, but loses his sight and an arm in the process – he is 'now helpless, indeed – blind and a cripple' (p. 477). The innkeeper tells her that he now lives alone at Ferndean Manor; she prepares to go there immediately.

Hearing her own story from the point of view of a disinterested observer is uncomfortable to Jane but interesting to us, as Rochester's deep love for her is reinforced by the tale of his behaviour after her disappearance. Also, his actions in the fire are admirable and go a long way to validating him as a good and noble man in our eyes, whereas before we may have been judging him harshly. However, Jane's sense and judgement have been so constantly and completely reinforced that by this stage in the **narrative** we can have little doubt that if she loves him so completely, he must be worthy of that love.

DID YOU KNOW?

Charlotte Brontë's own father was blind.

CHAPTER 37 – A third proposal accepted!

1 Jane is filled with pity on seeing Rochester.

2 They get to know one another again.

3 He proposes, and Jane accepts.

4 Rochester shows remorse for his past.

Jane's first sight of Rochester evokes pain and pity; he is a changed man, scarred both physically and emotionally by the events of the past year. She watches him for a while in secrecy, then announces herself at the house and surprises him in his living room. He cannot believe it is her: so many times has he dreamt of her return that he feels she is still a figment of his imagination. Although she has started out by teasing Rochester and keeping him at a distance for a while, she says simply, 'I am come back to you' (p. 482).

The next day is spent blissfully getting to know one another again. He questions her closely about her whereabouts, and shows some jealousy of St John. She puts his mind at rest on that score, and when he repeats his proposal to her, she accepts without hesitation.

DID YOU KNOW?

In 1854 Charlotte Brontë accepted her third offer of marriage and wed her father's curate.

He shows a great deal of remorse for his past actions and pride, and feels that God has inflicted a just series of punishments on him from which he has learned humility and repentance. When he thanks God for his fate and promises to 'lead henceforth a purer life than I have done hitherto!' (p. 497), we can rest assured that his life with Jane will be a happy one; that they both deserve and have earned contentment.

Jane's qualities and talents have always been undervalued, hidden to all except herself, the reader, and the few who deserve to appreciate them. They are less important in society's eyes than beauty, grace, money and social status. Therefore in her society she has always been unequal to those with whom she associates. Now, however, she is on equal status with Rochester: financially, physically and emotionally. This is very important to the future success of their relationship: note how uncomfortable she was with the engagement gifts he tried to heap on her, and how he now comments **ironically**: 'Never mind fine clothes and jewels, now: all that is not worth a fillip' (p. 495). Where once she was dependent upon him, they are now the same in every way.

CHAPTER 38 – The second Mrs Rochester

1 **Jane and Rochester marry.**

2 **They live a happy life.**

3 **We hear the details of the past ten years.**

The announcement of the wedding is made very simply and Jane and Rochester are married, quietly, without fuss, within the three days he promised. The final chapter calmly and simply describes their life together as one of sheer contentment and bliss: of a couple perfectly suited to each other in every respect.

The very last part of Jane's narration fills in details of the ten years that have passed. Adèle is placed in a good school by Jane, and grows into a fine young woman. Diana and Mary both marry good men and lead happy lives. Rochester regains the sight of his one eye, and is thus able to see his baby boy when he is born.

The story ends with St John Rivers: tireless devotion to his mission has weakened his health and Jane awaits news of his death, but does not weep for this. She knows that he is perfectly contented and joyous at the prospect of meeting his Maker.

> **CHECKPOINT 25**
>
> Why might Charlotte Brontë have allowed Rochester to regain sight in one eye?

Endings

The words 'Reader, I married him' (p. 498) are often assumed to be the final ones of the novel, and tend to overshadow the paragraphs about St John, which have significant status at the end of the story. This reinforces Christianity as one of the very important themes in the book, and makes it a book about religion as much as about romantic love.

Now take a break!

> **GLOSSARY**
>
> **a fillip** a click of the fingers

WHO SAYS ...?

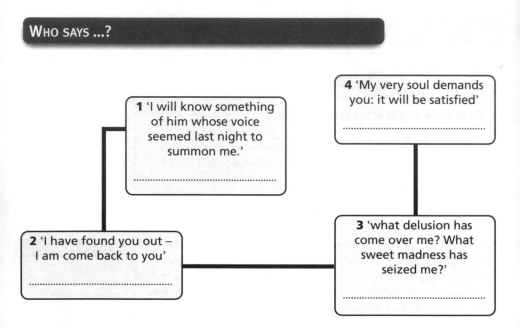

1 'I will know something of him whose voice seemed last night to summon me.'

....

2 'I have found you out – I am come back to you'

....

4 'My very soul demands you: it will be satisfied'

....

3 'what delusion has come over me? What sweet madness has seized me?'

....

ABOUT WHOM?

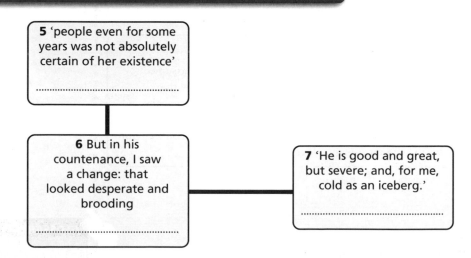

5 'people even for some years was not absolutely certain of her existence'

....

6 But in his countenance, I saw a change: that looked desperate and brooding

....

7 'He is good and great, but severe; and, for me, cold as an iceberg.'

....

Check your answers on p. 97.

PART THREE

COMMENTARY

THEMES

Although several of the major themes are discussed below, they are by no means a definitive list and it would be useful for you to consider how many others there are. It is often difficult to think about a theme in isolation and you will probably find that strands of a theme tend to overlap with each other.

ROMANCE

Jane Eyre is of course a love story and the relationship between Jane and Rochester is the main focus of the plot. On the surface Charlotte Brontë is making use of a very simple plot line which is familiar throughout the history of storytelling: boy meets girl, boy loses girl, boy and girl are reunited after some hardship and they all live happily ever after. This plot recurs again and again throughout all cultures and times.

Jane and Rochester are both passionate characters who have an enormous capacity to love. Neither one of them is physically attractive which is important because beauty often deflects attention away from character, which it must not do in their case. An important idea in the novel is that internal beauty is more important than external.

Jane and Rochester are clearly well suited, but have to be separated in order to experience an individual time of character development before they can finally enjoy peace together. Jane needs to become Rochester's equal in independence and maturity: her physical struggle and emotional torment strengthen her character and turn her into a woman rather than a naive girl. Rochester has committed a selfless act and proves that he has seen the error of his former ways in order to become a whole person again, now needing her as much as she needs him. Ironically, he is a better man without his sight and his arm than when he was whole, and Jane loves him better for being vulnerable than when he was fiercely independent. The nature of true love and marriage is examined in other relationships in the book:

CHECK THE BOOK
Wuthering Heights, by Charlotte's sister Emily, is another powerful and very dramatic love story.

- Aunt Reed's refusal to keep the promise made to her dead husband

- The scornful description of cousin Georgiana's 'advantageous match' (Ch. 22, p. 272)

- The prospect of a union between Rochester and Blanche Ingram, clearly good financially and socially, but not true love

- St John Rivers's love for Rosamund Oliver which is described as possibly a surface attraction: 'While something in me ... is acutely sensible to her charms, something else is as deeply impressed with her defects' (Ch. 32, p. 417)

- The prospect of a marriage of duty and convenience between Jane and St John, passionately rejected by the former: 'I scorn your idea of love... I scorn the counterfeit sentiment you offer' (Ch. 34, p. 454)

RELIGION

The nature of Christianity is explored in great detail throughout the novel, so much so that many people say it is as much a book about religion as it is a love story.

Religious ideas and images are referred to frequently and are an integral element of the novel. The religious context is significant because it was far more a part of everyone's day-to-day life than it is now. Nearly everyone went to church, said prayers at bedtime and studied the Bible.

DID YOU KNOW?

Charlotte Brontë's father was a parson.

Jane is extremely religious and comes across several characters who are also governed by their religious beliefs. Jane's system of value judgement is founded on a strict moral code. Think about examples in the text where she displays the following attributes:

- Putting others before herself and not being judgemental

- Valuing good character more highly than surface appearance

- Working hard to deserve the good opinion of others

There are several very 'religious' people in the novel. It is interesting to note Jane's reaction to each of them, and that whilst she can admire some and condemn others, she adheres to her own system of belief throughout. Think about her reaction to the following:

- Helen Burns, who displays the doctrine of 'turning the other cheek' constantly. She suffers terribly and never complains, even when unfairly treated

- Mr Brocklehurst, who is fearsome and tyrannical, and uses religion as a justification for cruelty and neglect

- Eliza Reed, a cold and fervent woman who gives her life to God by joining a nunnery. Jane views this with detached cynicism: 'You are not without sense, cousin Eliza; but what you have, I suppose in another year will be walled up alive in a French convent' (Ch. 22, p. 272)

- St John Rivers, a passionately religious man who is on a quest for the best way to give his life to God

In the end Jane chooses to believe that she is entitled to lead a happy life and that in doing so she can still serve God: 'if ever I thought a good thought – if ever I prayed a sincere and blameless prayer – if ever I wished a righteous wish, – I am rewarded now. To be your wife is, for me, to be as happy as I can be on earth' (Ch. 37, p. 494). She chooses a path similar to Miss Temple, Diana and Mary Rivers, which reinforces the rightness of her decision.

FEMALE INDEPENDENCE

Jane Eyre was written in 1847; therefore it is only just a few years into the Victorian period. Women had a very inferior status to men at this time, and few occupations were open to those who had to support themselves. Marriage was seen to be the only desirable goal, and was taken very seriously as a financial and business deal. Fathers gave their daughters large dowries when they married. Girls such as Jane had very few options open to them apart from using their education as a marketable resource.

This novel is often said to be a very political book because it explores the idea of a woman alone, in charge of her own life and making her own decisions. Jane could easily be described as a 'feminist'. She

EXAMINER'S SECRET

When using a quotation, write it exactly as it appears in the novel.

rejects the man she loves until such time as she can be his equal. She would rather be alone and independent than with Rochester on his terms (see p. 402).

Miss Temple, Diana and Mary Rivers all possess the values Jane admires. They all have to work for a living, and are therefore financially dependent on others. They all marry for love men who deserve them, rather than settling for financial security at the expense of happiness. Jane is very conscious that these women are not treated as they deserve to be: note the description of Miss Temple's reaction to being admonished by Mr Brocklehurst – 'she now gazed straight before her, and her face, naturally pale as marble, appeared to be assuming also the coldness and fixity of that material' (Ch. 7, p. 75). She hates the thought of Diana and Mary wasting their talents as governesses: 'by whose wealthy and haughty members they were regarded only as humble dependents, and who neither knew nor sought one of their innate excellences' (Ch. 30, p. 394). It is just as important for the novel to end comfortably by them finding happiness in an equal relationship.

Throughout her life Jane is placed in situations where she is dependent on others. She learns to keep her passionate and assertive side quiet except when driven to extremes: 'I never in my life have known any medium in my dealings with positive, hard characters, antagonistic to my own, between absolute submission and determined revolt' (Ch. 34, p. 446). Look again at three episodes which denote this clearly:

- Her outburst towards Mrs Reed in Chapter 4

- Her refusal of Rochester in Chapter 27

- Her refusal of St John during Chapters 34–5

EXAMINER'S SECRET
You will not get high marks simply by retelling the story.

Nonetheless, she is an assertive heroine. Look at the confidence and eloquence in her **dialogues** with Rochester from the start of their relationship. She is neither meek nor subservient with anyone; she often chooses to keep quiet rather than speak her mind unguardedly, but when called upon she is forthright and powerfully honest in her opinions.

This **theme** would not be complete without mention of the other strong female presence of the novel: Bertha Rochester. For a different perspective on her story it is worth considering the ideas in *The Wide Sargasso Sea* by Jean Rhys (1966). Many feminist interpretations of *Jane Eyre* have leapt to the defence of Bertha and used her to pronounce harsh judgement on Rochester. We never know if his account of their marriage and early years is true; we are given but one side of the story and there are several clues which help us begin to form a clearer judgement of the situation (see **Character**, of **Bertha**):

- Rochester views her as a malignant presence and uses devilish **imagery** in his descriptions of her.

- She never, however, attempts to harm anyone apart from him and herself, in spite of the opportunities she has to attack Jane.

- Her brother speaks of her with tenderness: 'Let her be taken care of; let her be treated as tenderly as may be' (Ch. 20, p. 242).

SOCIAL STATUS

Social status was very important in the nineteenth century. Class divisions were far more fixed and pronounced than they are today. In the novel, Jane is very conscious that, socially, she is inferior to many of those with whom she associates in spite of being a 'lady'. The idea that high social status does not necessarily mean goodness is an important **theme**

The existence of a strict and rigid class system is often referred to. Money dictates where one fits on the social ladder. The theme of respect being earned and not deserved due to one's bank balance is important.

In general, the characters seem to divide fairly easily into two categories – the rich landed gentry and the dependent classes who have to work to earn money. Think about the following in particular:

- Miss Ingram

- Rosamund Oliver

- Mrs Reed

? DID YOU KNOW?
'Madness' to the Georgian and Victorian often referred to anyone who did not adhere in the strictest terms to society's codes. Unmarried women, for instance, were often institutionalised for life.

- Miss Temple

- Diana and Mary Rivers

- Mrs Fairfax

- Georgiana Reed

- Jane

- Rochester

- St John Rivers

A useful exercise would be to find descriptions of each of these characters, and see if the rich are more or less admired than the dependent. It appears that Jane attaches very little value to wealth and does not see it as the road to any kind of happy life: look at her reaction to the prospect of owning a fortune in Chapter 33.

Although Jane is not rich she has been brought up to be ladylike and is therefore very different to the working-class farming people she associates with at Marsh End. Think about your reaction to her description of them 'Some of them are unmannered, rough, intractable, as well as ignorant; ... I must not forget that these coarsely clad little peasants are of flesh and blood as good as the scions of gentlest genealogy' (Ch. 31, p. 401). To us this can sound quite patronising, but remember that social status was fixed and people from one class mixed rarely with those of another, so Jane would be shocked at what she found.

Another example of the rigidity of social class is in the reaction to her parents' marriage: her mother was cast off for marrying someone from an 'inferior' class to herself. These societal forms and conventions were strictly adhered to in the nineteenth century.

STRUCTURE

The autobiographical form of *Jane Eyre* means that the novel follows a linear, chronological narrative. The idea of a journey through life is strongly highlighted by the five significant journeys that Jane takes.

Her personal journey has several purposes:

- From childhood to maturity

- From bondage to freedom

- From unhappiness to happiness

- From innocence to knowledge

Each phase of Jane's development is marked by a solitary journey. Note that Jane goes through severe tests at each stage: almost rites of passage, so that she can eventually deserve her happiness. It is only when she reaches her destination that the journey is at an end – which is marked by her settling at Ferndean Manor for life.

There are five general 'sections' to the novel:

❶ Jane's childhood at Gateshead

❷ Her school years

❸ Time at Thornfield

❹ Marsh End

❺ The conclusion or 'happy ending'

Although the novel covers the whole of Jane's life, only the most dramatic two years are dwelt upon in detail. The Thornfield section is the longest in spite of being the shortest period of time: seventeen chapters out of a total thirty-eight are devoted to this period. This marks it as the most important phase of Jane's life, as well as the most interesting to the reader.

CHARACTERS

JANE

Jane Eyre is the eponymous heroine of the novel. Strong willed and passionate, her search for true love and happiness forms the story of the novel. She has a well-developed sense of right and wrong from an early age. She is a very good judge of character as a child, warming

DID YOU KNOW?

Jane Eyre tells her story ten years after the last event in the novel, her arrrival in Ferndean.

Small but strong-willed

Financially dependent but independent of spirit

Shy but passionate

instantly to Miss Temple and Helen Burns, whilst loathing Mrs Reed and Mr Brocklehurst.

Her strong personal integrity is a marked feature of her personality. She is aware that she is penniless and alone in the world and has to be very independent. She may be naive and innocent but she is able to look after herself very well. Twice in her life she has to make very difficult choices, one to leave Mr Rochester and the other to reject St John Rivers. On both these occasions she is faced with very strong-willed characters, but she masters both of them and has her own way. People are of paramount importance to her but she retains her independence of mind in spite of her need to be accepted and loved. Her search is for unconditional acceptance, and she sacrifices nothing of herself in her relationships with others.

There is a passionate woman hidden underneath Jane's shy and deferential appearance. She is deeply religious, and her faith in God is at times the only thing which sustains her. However, she refuses to accept the belief of Helen Burns and St John Rivers that she should sacrifice happiness on earth in order to get to heaven. She wants happiness now, and eventually gets everything she deserves.

ROCHESTER

Mr Rochester is a fascinating, romantic figure. He is a very unhappy man when we first meet him. At a very young age his father and elder brother tricked him into his marriage with Bertha Mason in order that he should get her dowry of £30,000. When he discovers that she is insane he has to bear the responsibility of this alone, and only brings her to Thornfield Hall when his brother dies and the house is left to him. He then runs away abroad to try to forget his troubles by leading an immoral life, but the knowledge of Bertha's existence haunts him and his shady life only helps to turn him bitter.

Romantic and arrogant

Lonely and passionate

Immoral and responsible

His pure love for Jane eventually changes him back to the man he was, but his actions towards her have often been judged very harshly. He does attempt to marry her illegally, but we feel such sympathy for his predicament and his immense love for Jane that his actions can be understood. He is a man who believes he is doing the best he can for his mad wife, although locking a woman in one windowless room for ten years with a drunkard for a keeper is a questionable way of doing the right thing.

He redeems himself by his actions in the fire which destroys Thornfield, as well as by appreciating and loving Jane. He is only allowed contentment after he has suffered and recognised 'the error of his ways': 'I began to see and acknowledge the hand of God in my doom. I began to experience remorse, repentance; the wish for reconcilement to my Maker' (Ch. 37, p. 495). His blinded and crippled state is a **metaphor** for his loss of arrogance and pride. We feel that he is now worthy of the love Jane feels for him, and indeed it would have been difficult for her to be equally matched with someone less passionate and forceful than herself.

BERTHA

The first Mrs Rochester, or 'the madwoman in the attic', is an intriguing subject. She is an elusive figure who never speaks and is seen only twice, and yet she dominates the central action of the novel. Her presence is felt powerfully from the moment Jane enters Thornfield: 'It was a curious laugh; distinct, formal, mirthless' (Ch. 11, p. 122).

Her actions are dramatic and violent, and very interesting to interpret. She attacks Rochester twice, once by attempting to burn his bed, and second by flying at him when he presents her to Jane and the others. She attacks her brother when he comes to visit her. She tears Jane's wedding veil the night before her marriage. And her final act before her suicide is to set fire to Jane's bed.

Insane

Cunning

Hidden yet ever-present

We have to accept that she is believed to be insane because that is what we are told. Rochester is vague on the subject of her illness and makes the problem sound more like a difference in character and temperament than insanity. Moreover, her actions do seem to suggest that she is aware of what is going on at Thornfield, which makes us wonder what kind of insanity she is suffering from. Could she be a woman driven to madness by an unsympathetic husband? There is an implicit jealousy of Jane in her actions, or at least her position as recipient of Rochester's love. She manifests great anger towards her husband: maybe because she loves him, or because he has kept her shut away for so long. However we choose to interpret her character and motives, she is not to be ignored as a side-issue in the novel.

ST JOHN

St John Rivers is a religious fanatic. He is young and handsome, very intelligent and well-educated. His religious conviction goes beyond that of all his close associates, including his sisters and Jane, and becomes the dominant force of his personality.

**Fanatical and cold
Inflexible and
altruistic**

During the nineteenth century many deeply religious people went to third-world countries to bring Christianity to the 'heathens'. It was from this source that much of the world was converted to Christianity. It seems quite an arrogant idea to place Christianity above any other religion, but it is important to remember that people such as St John were convinced that you could only be 'saved' if you were a Christian.

The problem with St John is that his beliefs are so profound and inflexible that he allows for no human faults, and this makes him an austere character. Jane clearly struggles with this aspect of him, because she can see his kindness in his devotion to helping others no matter what the personal sacrifice. Jane believes that she can serve God by enjoying the life that He gave her, whereas St John believes that the only way to ensure a place in heaven is to devote your life to others at the expense of your own comfort and happiness.

MRS REED

Cruel guardian

Jane's aunt Reed is her guardian. Jane spends ten unhappy years in her house with her three objectionable children, John, Eliza and Georgiana. Mrs Reed is clearly a stern and cold woman who has no feelings for Jane at all and makes no effort to get along with her, in spite of promises made to her dead husband to raise her as a daughter.

She is evidently relieved to ship Jane off to school, and makes no further contact with her until Jane is an adult and Mrs Reed is on her deathbed. She hates Jane so much that she tells Jane's uncle she is dead rather than give her whereabouts. Family disgrace and financial ruin seem to be fitting punishments for so cruel a woman, but Jane forgives her. In spite of being close to death she refuses to be reconciled with

Jane, indeed managing to blame her for the dreadful act: 'You were born, I think, to be my torment: my last hour is racked by the recollection of a deed, which, but for you, I should never have been tempted to commit' (Ch. 21, p. 268). Her function in the novel is important for two reasons: little Jane is able to show how she responds to senseless cruelty, and the adult Jane is able to demonstrate her lack of vindictiveness: 'I long earnestly to be reconciled to you now: kiss me, aunt' (Ch. 21, p. 269).

HELEN

Helen Burns is another pupil at Lowood school. Jane is instantly drawn to her when she arrives there. Helen's illness is announced before we even meet her: 'the sound of a cough close behind me, made me turn my head' (Ch. 5, p. 59). She is to have a profound effect on Jane's life in many ways. She is the first person ever to be consistently kind to Jane – her first friend, in fact. She is clearly very intelligent and well read: qualities Jane admires very much as they lead to independence of mind.

Jane's first friend
Intelligent
True Christian
Dies

She is a Christian in the true sense of the word. She believes that it is her duty to suffer patiently whatever punishment she is given. Jane reacts strongly to this: 'I could not comprehend this doctrine of endurance' (Ch. 6, p. 66).

Jane does not know that Helen is very ill, although her coughing would have alerted the contemporary reader to the fact that she has tuberculosis, a common disease at that time. Her death affects Jane so profoundly that she never mentions her again, although we know that she visits her grave fifteen years later and erects the gravestone in her memory. Helen's function is to give Jane a friend and ally at Lowood, and to introduce the ideas of religious sacrifice which run through the novel.

MISS TEMPLE

As superintendent of Lowood School, Miss Temple is Jane's teacher for six years and friend for two, serving as a role model in many respects: 'to her instruction I owed the best part of my acquirements; her friendship and society had been my continual solace; she had

Role model

Cruel clergyman
Un-Christian
Hypocrite

stood me in the stead of mother, governess, and latterly, companion' (Ch. 10, p. 98). She is clearly a very good teacher, knowledgeable and intelligent as well as kind and fair. Her effect is so strong that when she leaves Lowood to be married Jane feels the loss of 'the serene atmosphere I had been breathing in her vicinity' (Ch. 10, p. 99).

She stands up to Mr Brocklehurst and defends the girls against his strict regime. He is a fearsome man as well as her superior, and yet she is not afraid to defend the children when she feels he is inflicting too much unnecessary suffering.

MR BROCKLEHURST

The clergyman in charge of Lowood, Mr Brocklehurst is Jane's first experience of a religious person. He is harsh and austere, and uses religion as a justification for treating the girls at Lowood cruelly. He is a hypocrite, however, because although he advocates physical suffering for the girls, his wife and daughters are allowed to wear fancy clothes and rich jewels. His regime is partially to blame for so many of the girls dying of typhus fever, and there is a strong sense of relief when his charge of the school is taken away from him.

He is clearly an acquaintance of Mrs Reed; this is a strong indicator that he is not a pleasant man, because we already know enough of her character to assume that anyone she admires will not be a nice person.

MRS FAIRFAX

Alice Fairfax is the matronly housekeeper of Thornfield Hall. She is a distant relation of the Rochesters and a trusted employee. She has a great deal of common sense, and Jane respects her very much. She is Jane's second mother figure (after Miss Temple) and Jane admires her discretion as well as occasionally despairing of it.

Placid and kind

She is somewhat baffled by Rochester's relationship with Jane, and is very concerned about the proposed marriage. Although this is never made clear, it is possible that she knows the real identity of 'the madwoman in the attic', and this is why she warns Jane to take care.

Jane is uncomfortable with this warning but it is meant kindly and has much truth in it.

GRACE POOLE

Mrs Poole is a servant, hired to keep charge of Bertha. Her presence at Thornfield Hall is used to explain the strange noises and events that Jane witnesses. She appears contented in her strange, isolated occupation.

Grace drinks too much; Rochester mentions her temporary lapses of memory by which he means alcoholic stupors. This is possibly excusable, given the circumstances of her life. She has developed a close relationship with Bertha and understands her very well.

Alcoholic servant

Responsible for Bertha

DIANA AND MARY RIVERS

The sisters of St John are to become Jane's sisters in mind if not in blood tie, although it transpires that they are related. They are very similar to Jane: educated, interesting, kind and gentle. Jane blossoms in their company, becoming more relaxed and confident because she is liked and respected by those whom she likes and respects. They have a significant function in aiding Jane to reach maturity and complete her sense of self.

Sister figures

MISS INGRAM

Blanche Ingram is everything that Jane is not: of a titled, wealthy family, majestic and beautiful, self-confident and with all the social graces. She appears to be the perfect match for Mr Rochester, or so poor Jane thinks, and Mr Rochester teasingly allows her and us readers to continue to believe this, thus making Jane's love for him appear all the more poignant, and keeping us readers in suspense. However, though Blanche may have a superficial cleverness, she is also arrogant, vain and with a touch of malice. She is no match, in Mr Rochester's eyes, for Jane's intellect, modesty and pragmatism; indeed, she is not to Mr Rochester's taste at all. She is as loud and brash as Jane is deferential. In many ways they are polar opposites of each other.

Beautiful and self-possessed

Arrogant and malicious

LANGUAGE AND STYLE

STYLE AND LANGUAGE CHOICES

A writer's style is simply the way he or she uses words. The language used by a writer is the end-product of a range of choices which are based on the purpose of the writing.

EXAMINER'S SECRET

If the rubric gives planning time, **use it** to plan your answers!

Jane Eyre was published in the Victorian period when attitudes were very strict. The novel depicts a good woman who is capable of strong emotion and passion. Her first encounter with Mr Rochester establishes the ultimate pattern of their relationship, the wounded man tended by a devoted woman, but she is at pains to point out that beauty in masculine form is not important to her: 'I ... should have shunned (it) as one would fire, lightning, or anything else that is bright' (Ch. 12, p. 130). For all that, her description of him reveals the way she is stirred by his essential maleness: having noted his 'considerable breadth of chest' (Ch. 12, p. 129), she observes his 'dark face, with stern features and a heavy brow' (Ch. 12, p. 129) and comments finally that 'the roughness of the traveller set me at my ease' (Ch. 12, p. 130). Rochester, as the language reveals, clearly is a man capable of stirring this young woman's emotion and passions.

AUTOBIOGRAPHY

The facsimile of the frontispiece to the first edition of this novel describes it: '*Jane Eyre*: an Autobiography, edited by Currer Bell'. The book is not, however, an autobiography but a work of fiction. And of course Jane Eyre is not a real person, but a character existing in a narrative. However, the novel is highly reminiscent of an autobiography. It is narrated in the first person, thereby immediately drawing the reader into a closer sense of identification with the central character, and implicitly creating more of a sense of realism. Also, as twentieth-first-century readers, we have knowledge about the author unknown to the contemporary readership. We know that many details of the work were drawn directly from the author's personal experience. Many characters, situations and places are taken from her own life. And the eponymous heroine bears, in many respects, a startling resemblance to Charlotte Brontë herself. Although not completely autobiographical, this novel is not completely fictional either.

'READER'

Jane constantly addresses her 'reader' directly: 'Reader, I married him' (Ch. 38, p. 498). This draws attention to the fact that there is a narrator here telling a story, but we are invited to believe it is real: 'whether what followed was the effect of excitement, the reader shall judge' (Ch. 35, p. 466). To a certain extent Brontë was following literary convention by exploring the use of narrative stance in storytelling. For example, she often shifts between past and present tense for different effects. Her heroine is not an omniscient narrator; therefore, the reader is able to see things that Jane cannot, and participate in the story: we have an overview which she doesn't share.

LANGUAGE

The language of the novel is very difficult to someone unfamiliar with nineteenth-century texts. The sentences are long and complicated, and the vocabulary is elaborate. This formal prose was very common at this time, in spoken and written language. However, the very nature of some of the language highlights that Jane is an articulate, intelligent woman, whose language reflects her learning.

Names

Charlotte Brontë wrote very carefully and took great care with small details, including the choice of names. 'Eyre', for example, came from the Eyre family whose house had a room in it which had housed a madwoman. The name was also chosen because it had the sense of being as 'free as air'. The name 'Temple' suggests a place of worship, safety and goodness. 'Jane' hints at 'plain Jane'.

Dialect

There are times when Yorkshire dialect is included in the text. These are not always easy for us to follow. Dialect, like colloquial language, is often used to show characters of a lower social class. For example, Hannah, the servant in the Rivers household, speaks in strong dialect, which is represented in the text: 'You look a raight down dacent little crater' (Ch. 29, p. 383). In the twenty-first century, the accent remains though the dialect itself is passing into disuse as people are exposed to the common language of the mass media – television, radio and pop music, for example. Hannah's conversation (Ch. 29, pp. 382–4)

EXAMINER'S SECRET
You've heard it before, but we'll say it again: always read the question paper carefully before you start answering anything.

contains very few dialect words but it is sufficient to establish that she is a member of the servant class, outspoken but possessed of shrewd judgement.

When she realises that Jane is sincerely in difficult circumstances, her bluntness gives way to friendship: 'She put her floury ... hand into mine ... and from that moment we were friends' (Ch. 29, p. 383). One is tempted to observe that Hannah's language is as 'floury' as her hands! The plainness of her expression reveals a practical, down-to-earth character with a respect for truth and honesty.

EXAMINER'S SECRET
An A-grade candidate can analyse a variety of the writer's techniques.

Descriptive language

The descriptive passages of the novel draw us into the action. Their style is often quite journalistic:

> It was the fifteenth of January, about nine o'clock in the morning: Bessie was gone down to breakfast; my cousins had not yet been summoned to their mama.   (Ch. 4, p. 38)

However, these descriptive passages can also be highly suggestive:

> Terrible moment: full of struggle, blackness, burning! Not a human being that ever lived could wish to be loved better than I was loved; and him who thus loved me I absolutely worshipped: and I must renounce love and idol.   (Ch. 27, p. 354)

Dialogue

Dialogue enables us to hear the characters actually speaking to each other and Brontë uses it for a variety of purposes. At the beginning of Chapter 11 (p. 108) she remarks, 'A new chapter in a novel is something like a new scene in a play.' This is a significant observation since she tends to use dialogue in this dramatic way. Through it she is able to convey the social station and attitude of the characters. Since most of the story is told in the first person, we are always aware of what Jane is thinking and feeling but how can we arrive at the feelings and thoughts of others? One of the most direct ways is naturally through listening to them talk as we do when a scene is dramatised.

This is clearly illustrated in Chapter 27 (p. 355) when Jane realises she cannot marry Rochester and the accompanying actions are enclosed in brackets as though they were stage directions:

'Jane, do you mean to go one way ... and to let me no another?'

'I do.'

'Jane' (bending towards and embracing me), 'do you mean it now?'

Elsewhere the dialogue is used to reveal aspects of character. Notice (Chapter 6, p. 66) the measured language of the saintly Helen Burns as she explains her attitude to being unfairly flogged by Miss Scatcherd. When Jane remarks that she personally could not have endured it passively, Helen says, 'It is far better to endure patiently a smart which nobody feels but yourself, than to commit a hasty action whose evil consequences will extend to all connected with you.'

Language of feelings

The language of the novel is most powerful when it describes Jane's torment. Jane's descriptions of what is going on in her own mind are very striking and we feel closer to Jane because we see events from her point of view. Her feelings, especially her 'conscience' and her 'passion', are often given their own voice, and seem to fight over her right to decide her own actions. In Chapter 27, when Jane makes the decision to leave Rochester, we see this very clearly. Jane's passion for Rochester makes her want to stay, but her conscience tells her she should leave. This style helps us to understand what Jane is going through, and to understand why she acts as she does.

www. **CHECK THE NET**
www.vanderbilt. edu is a very useful American college website

Now take a break!

PART FOUR

RESOURCES

HOW TO USE QUOTATIONS

One of the secrets of success in writing essays is the way you use quotations. There are five basic principles:

❶ Put inverted commas at the beginning and end of the quotation.

❷ Write the quotation exactly as it appears in the original.

❸ Do not use a quotation that repeats what you have just written.

❹ Use the quotation so that it fits into your sentence.

❺ Keep the quotation as short as possible.

EXAMINER'S SECRET

In a typical examination you might use as many as eight quotations.

Quotations should be used to develop the line of thought in your essays. Your comment should not duplicate what is in your quotation. For example:

> **Jane is devastated at the idea of having to leave Thornfield:**
> 'I see the necessity of departure; and it is like looking on the necessity of death' (Ch. 23, p. 283)

Far more effective is to write:

> **Jane sees how important it is for her to leave Thornfield, although it feels like** 'the necessity of death'. (Ch. 23, p. 283)

The most sophisticated way of using the writer's words is to embed them into your sentence:

> **Jane is struck** 'with terror and anguish' (Ch. 23, p. 283) **at the idea of leaving Thornfield for ever.**

When you use quotations in this way, you are demonstrating the ability to use text as evidence to support your ideas – not simply including words from the original to prove you have read it.

COURSEWORK ESSAY

Set aside an hour or so at the start of your work to plan what you have to do.

- List all the points you feel are needed to cover the task. Collect page references of information and quotations that will support what you have to say. A helpful tool is the highlighter pen: this saves painstaking copying and enables you to target precisely what you want to use.

- Focus on what you consider to be the main points of the essay. Try to sum up your argument in a single sentence, which could be the closing sentence of your essay. Depending on the essay title, it could be a statement about a character: The essence of Jane's character is that she retains her independence of spirit and triumphs over repression and cruelty; an opinion about setting: The author continually emphasises mood and theme by stressing the importance of external surroundings; or a judgement on a theme: *Jane Eyre* remains a fascinating and popular novel because the theme of romantic love is just as relevant today as it has ever been.

- Make a short essay plan. Use the first paragraph to introduce the argument you wish to make. In the following paragraphs develop this argument with details, examples and other possible points of view. Sum up your argument in the last paragraph. Check you have answered the question.

- Write the essay, remembering all the time the central point you are making.

- On completion, go back over what you have written to eliminate careless errors and improve expression. Read it aloud to yourself, or, if you are feeling more confident, to a relative or friend.

If you can, try to type your essay using a word processor. This will allow you to correct and improve your writing without spoiling its appearance.

EXAMINER'S SECRET

Examiners **never** take marks away.

SITTING THE EXAMINATION

Examination papers are carefully designed to give you the opportunity to do your best. Follow these handy hints for exam success:

BEFORE YOU START

EXAMINER'S SECRET

Always read the whole examination paper before you start writing.

- Make sure you know the subject of the examination so that you are properly prepared and equipped.

- You need to be comfortable and free from distractions. Inform the invigilator if anything is off-putting, e.g. a shaky desk.

- Read the instructions, or rubric, on the front of the examination paper. You should know by now what you have to do but check to reassure yourself.

- Observe the time allocation – and follow it carefully. If they recommend 60 minutes for Question 1 and 30 minutes for Question 2, it is because Question 1 carries twice as many marks.

- Consider the mark allocation. You should write a longer response for 4 marks than for 2 marks.

WRITING YOUR RESPONSES

- Use the questions to structure your response, e.g. question: 'The endings of X's poems are always particularly significant. Explain their importance with reference to two poems.' The first part of your answer will describe the ending of the first poem; the second part will look at the ending of the second poem; the third part will be an explanation of the significance of the two endings.

- Write a brief draft outline of your response.

- A typical 30-minute examination essay is probably between 400 and 600 words in length.

- Keep your writing legible and easy to read, using paragraphs to show the structure of your answers.

- Spend a couple of minutes afterwards quickly checking for obvious errors.

WHEN YOU HAVE FINISHED

- Don't be downhearted – if you found the examination difficult, it is probably because you really worked at the questions. Let's face it, they are not meant to be easy!

- Don't pay too much attention to what your friends have to say about the paper. Everyone's experience is different and no two people ever give the same answers.

IMPROVE YOUR GRADE

Your potential grades in any examination can be improved. An examiner marks your work according to a mark scheme that is applied equally to all candidates and no examiner knows in advance your level of achievement. All candidates start at the same point: a blank answer booklet.

This booklet is considered by the exam board to give more than enough space for the candidate to achieve the highest marks so there is no need for you to rush to fill up three or four extra sheets. It might look impressive to your friends to see you covering reams of paper but the chances are that you will be doing a fair amount of writing that is not relevant. Moreover, the two hours your examination is scheduled to last is long enough for you to gain the highest marks without rushing.

So take your time, think carefully, plan carefully, write carefully and check carefully. A relaxed performer always works best – in any field and in every examination!

Whatever you are studying, the way to be completely relaxed in an examination is to know your subject inside out. There is no substitute for reading and re-reading the text.

We have divided the story summaries in these York Notes on *Jane Eyre* into five sections and in your study strategy you can make use of these divisions. Using a single sheet for each section, list what happens

EXAMINER'S SECRET

If you are asked to make a comparison, use comparing words such as 'on the other hand', 'however' and 'by contrast'.

EXAMINER'S SECRET

Always have a spare pen!

in the story. This approach enables you to be familiar with the precise sequence of events.

Do the same with the characters, devoting a single sheet to each of them: who they are, what they do and what they say. Back up these notes with short relevant quotations. These can be used to build up a character study or to support comments you make in an essay.

You may be allowed to take the novel into the examination hall but reference to it may well cost you valuable time unless you know it thoroughly. Your notes on plot and character are the ideal last-minute revision aids.

You will almost certainly know more than enough to secure a high grade; the important thing is to make the most of what you have learnt.

The main reason candidates let themselves down is that they *fail to read the question*! Do not begin writing until you are sure you know what you want to say because it is very easy to lose track and end up writing off the subject. Whilst you are writing, it is a good idea to check back occasionally and make sure you are still answering the question.

Keep an eye on the clock. Most literature papers want you to answer two questions in two hours. It may seem obvious but it is worth reminding yourself that you need to spend about an hour on each answer. Avoid the temptation of writing for too long on the question you enjoy and thereby stealing time from the other question! Your final result will depend on getting decent marks for *both* questions.

Read the notes given below that describe what examiners are looking for in different quality responses and apply them to your own work.

IMPROVING YOUR RESPONSE FROM A D TO A C

- Instead of writing, '**Rochester looks a broken man**', you would write, '**Rochester is very much the same man that she always knew except that now she sees him as a "sightless Samson"'** (Ch. 37, p. 479).

- Instead of putting in a number of quotations to describe his physical appearance, concentrate on her reaction to him, noting that she felt 'A soft hope ... (that she) should dare to drop a soft kiss on that brow of rock' (Ch. 37, p. 479–80).

- Instead of noting that he trusted no one in his changed circumstances, illustrate your point by observing that even his trusted dog, Pilot, kept out of his way for fear of being 'inadvertently trodden upon' (Ch. 37, p. 481).

EXAMINER'S SECRET

A short quotation is always more effective than a lengthy one.

IMPROVING YOUR RESPONSE FROM A C TO A B

- Instead of writing that **'Rochester believes Jane will marry St John'**, describe the jealousy that he feels for the man, that he in comparison feels himself to be 'hideous' (Ch. 37, p. 486) nothing but a 'sightless block' (Ch. 37, p. 484).

- Instead of putting in a couple of quotations, use detail from the whole chapter that collectively creates a sense of St John's being a very attractive man in a variety of ways but still Jane cannot love him as she does Rochester. For all that St John has a 'first-rate' (Ch. 37, p. 489) brain, is 'untiringly active' (Ch. 37, p. 489), 'dresses well' (Ch. 37, p. 490) and is 'handsome', (Ch. 37, p. 490), Jane prefers Rochester.

- Instead of commenting that the writer uses similes or metaphors, comparing Rochester to 'a lion, or something of that sort' (Ch. 37, p. 484), you could indicate that she uses a range of expressions to create the impression that Rochester, though blinded and mutilated, has lost none of his strength and appeal, as she observes 'the powerlessness of the strong man touched my heart to the quick' (Ch. 37, p. 488).

IMPROVING YOUR RESPONSE FROM A B TO AN A

- Instead of just observing how Jane and Rochester feel (for example, Jane's immediate attraction to Rochester when she sees him standing on the front doorstep, her 'rapture ... kept well in check by pain' (Ch. 37, p. 479) or Rochester's 'sweet madness' (Ch. 37, p. 482) when he realises Jane is in the room with him), you can show how you share their feelings and can empathise with their reactions to each other's presence.

- You could identify the classical references Charlotte Brontë uses, that he is variously compared with 'Samson' (Ch. 37, p. 490), 'Nebuchadnezzar' (Ch. 37, p. 490) and the lame blacksmith god 'Vulcan' (Ch. 37, p. 490), and comment that one effect of this is to elevate Rochester to heroic status.

- Instead of just using references to illustrate the various stages of their reconciliation, you now present a line of thought about the enduring nature of their love with quotations to secure your argument, 'Reader, I married him' (Ch. 38, p. 498), being intended for the female reader who would understand precisely how, despite closely adhering to all the rules regarding propriety in the conduct of a love affair, she caught Rochester's heart and made him her own!

- Instead of observing the techniques used by the author, you start to analyse how the characters' thoughts and feelings are enhanced by Charlotte Brontë's use of language. Rochester's language is angry – he is abusive towards St John, muttering 'damn him' (Ch. 37, p. 490) when Jane's praise of that man seems too strong – and full of dark doubts, 'expecting nothing', (Ch. 37, p. 486) whilst Jane is hesitant, believing only that she has 'the means of fretting him out of his melancholy' (Ch. 37, p. 487), but not much more than that. She does not wish to seem too forward but tries to lead him into a realisation that her love for him remains as strong as ever and that she desperately wants to marry him! 'Choose then, sir,' she finally says, '– her who loves you best?' (Ch. 37, p. 494). Even the dullest of men could not fail to spot the italics are aimed at him!

When you have finished, take a final look through what you have written. This is not an enjoyable experience for any candidate but it is a necessary process. You have been working under considerable pressure, exactly the conditions that produce silly errors. Now is your final chance to put your words in order before they disappear into the examination system along with thousands of other examination papers.

SAMPLE ESSAY PLAN

The following essay plan will show you how to structure an essay and will provide you with some ideas on the following question. It is divided into six parts and the points below have been made in note form. This is only one possible plan. You may well have your own ideas.

EXAMINER'S SECRET
You are always given credit for writing your essay plans.

> In what ways is the idea of 'journey' significant to the understanding of *Jane Eyre*?

Part 1

Introduce your essay with a general discussion of the five actual journeys that Jane makes during the book, and also introduce the idea that the whole novel is a journey through life for her from childhood innocence to adult maturity.

Part 2

Look in more detail at each of the journeys:

- From Gateshead to Lowood
- From Lowood to Thornfield
- From Gateshead to Thornfield
- From Thornfield to Marsh End
- From Marsh End to Thornfield

Discuss the elements of each – happy or unhappy – what mood she is in, looking forward or back, aware of what she is journeying towards or going into the unknown, etc. Examine the ways in which she is shown to be less vulnerable every time she makes a journey.

Part 3

Now look at the 'figurative' journey in the book. Think about:

- Childhood to adulthood
- Innocence to maturity

- Unhappiness to happiness
- Servitude to freedom

Part 4

Conclude by bringing the two ideas together in a paragraph which summarises the ideas, and commenting on the way the literal journeys highlight the central idea of the whole book being a journey. You could mention something about Jane finally reaching her 'destination' in Chapter 38, which is why she writes in the present tense rather than looking back into the past.

Further questions

1. How are the ideas about 'home' and 'belonging' shown to be important in the story of *Jane Eyre*?

2. Look at Jane's attitude towards Adèle Varens, Blanche Ingram and Diana and Mary Rivers. How do her responses to these characters affect our understanding of her?

3. Discuss the use of weather in the text, with reference to at least three specific occasions.

4. How does Jane's attitude to Gateshead, Thornfield and Moor House highlight her feelings about wealth?

5. Look again at the development of the relationship between Jane and Rochester. What is it that makes her fall in love with him?

6. Re-read the passages in Chapters 15 and 27 where Rochester tells Jane about his early life. What judgements are we being asked to make about his character from this information?

7. How are ideas about religion examined through the characters of Mr Brocklehurst, Eliza Reed and St John Rivers?

8. Carefully reread the information about Bertha Rochester in Chapters 26, 27 and 37. Why might Rochester's viewpoint be different to that of the reader?

9 How do Jane's childhood experiences at Gateshead and Lowood help to form her character?

10 Discuss the theme of romantic love in *Jane Eyre*. Illustrate your answer with reference to her rejection of St John Rivers and acceptance of Rochester.

EXAMINER'S SECRET

Everything you write on your answer sheet is marked.

Now take a break!

**THE LEARNING CENTRE
TOWER HAMLETS COLLEGE
ARBOUR SQUARE
LONDON E1 0PS**

atmosphere mood – sometimes external, sometimes internal

chronological a style of narrative where the events are ordered in time sequence

dialect regional variations in the use of standard English

dialogue the speech or conversation of characters

eponymous the person whose name is used as the title of the book

genre a 'kind' or 'type' of literature

Gothic a story of cruel passions and supernatural terrors usually in a medieval setting

image mental picture created with words

imagery figurative language including metaphors and similes

irony the use of words to convey the opposite of their literal meaning; incongruity between what might be expected and what actually occurs

linear similar to chronological – following a straightforward sequence of events

metaphor a descriptive device which states that one thing is another, figuratively rather than literally

narrative the story

narrator the person telling the story, maybe involved or impartial to the story

omniscient literally all-knowing – a type of narrator who knows more about the story than the characters

pathetic fallacy a way of emphasising mood by linking it to the surrounding world

pathos moments which evoke strong feelings of pity or sadness

personification attributing human characteristics to an objeect or animal

present tense writing as if experiencing events at that very moment

prose writing not in verse or any other kind of structure

subtext the situation that lies behind the characters or events which may never be directly referred to

theme the central ideas of the novel rather than merely the plot

CHECKPOINT 1 He is concerned about her misery, identifies the cause of her depression and suggests that she is sent away to school.

CHECKPOINT 2 A feeling that she is isolated creates sympathy for the character.

CHECKPOINT 3 It adds to the impression we form of the harsh conditions endured by the girls at Lowood.

CHECKPOINT 4 Jane's appearance contrasts strongly with that of the other women: her dress is shabby whilst theirs is sumptuous, yet she is condemned for vanity because of her naturally curly hair.

CHECKPOINT 5 It is a conversation involving solely women that is both intelligent and warm.

CHECKPOINT 6 Jane is in no way judgemental about the faults Adèle reveals.

CHECKPOINT 7 Despite the delay in meeting him and his less than friendly manner, Jane feels instantly at ease with him.

CHECKPOINT 8 She feels he is attracted to her but when she learns that he will be meeting Blanche Ingram, she tries to get a sense of perspective about the situation, by painting two miniatures, an unflattering one of herself and a beautiful one of Blanche.

CHECKPOINT 9 She is prepared to accept that Rochester might prefer Blanche to her but is worried that he may marry a woman who is cruel to others and cold in nature.

CHECKPOINT 10 Where the other women react hysterically, Jane is resourceful and measured in her response.

CHECKPOINT 11 She finally realises that she is deeply in love with Rochester yet is able to accept the pain she will feel when he does marry another woman.

CHECKPOINT 12 You would have expected her to enjoy having him spend money on her but she feels the need to be independent and writes to her uncle for financial help.

CHECKPOINT 13 Quite simply, she trusts him and wants to believe in him.

CHECKPOINT 14 He loves her and she loves him but she cannot bring herself to act in a way that is morally wrong.

CHECKPOINT 15 Because she is metaphorically travelling into another phase in her life.

CHECKPOINT 16 The candle may be seen as a sign of hope: it may be tiny and it may be flickering but it represents the possibility of help and safety.

CHECKPOINT 17 It shows a delicacy and respect for privacy which Jane certainly empathises with.

CHECKPOINT 18 St John has devoted his life to God but it has not necessarily made him happy. Jane has left Rochester out of a sense of duty to a higher being but it has not made her happy either!

CHECKPOINT 19 Money is often a useful dramatic device in order to assist plot resolution.

CHECKPOINT 20 It may not have replaced the life she wanted as the wife of Rochester but at least she feels she is doing the right thing.

CHECKPOINT 21 She enables us to see the extent to which St John Rivers will sacrifice personal happiness for a higher cause.

CHECKPOINT 22 Her ready generosity is another example of her exemplary fairness and sense of moral justice.

CHECKPOINT 23 She is keen to please them because she admires them, a regular feature of Jane's behaviour.

CHECKPOINT 24 She is now a confident adult. Quite clear about what she wants from life, her every action is governed by her desire to marry Rochester.

CHECKPOINT 25 He has paid for his past transgressions, so the partial regaining of sight signals a sort of forgiveness. He is also thereby empowered to become a better father and husband since he can see his infant son and fully express his love for Jane as mother of his child.

TEST YOURSELF (CHAPTERS 1–4)

1 Mrs Reed *(Chapter 1)*

2 Mr Lloyd *(Chapter 3)*

3 Jane *(Chapter 4)*

4 Mr Brocklehurst *(Chapter 4)*

5 Jane *(Chapter 3)*

6 Mr Brocklehurst *(Chapter 4)*

7 Jane *(Chapter 4)*

TEST YOURSELF (CHAPTERS 5–10)

1 Miss Temple *(Chapter 5)*

2 Helen Burns *(Chapter 5)*

3 Helen Burns *(Chapter 6)*

4 Mr Brocklehurst *(Chapter 7)*

5 Bessie Leaven *(Chapter 10)*

6 Helen Burns *(Chapter 6)*

7 Miss Temple *(Chapter 6)*

8 Jane *(Chapter 7)*

TEST YOURSELF (CHAPTERS 11–27)

1 Mrs Fairfax *(Chapter 11)*

2 Mr Rochester *(Chapter 12)*

3 Mr Rochester *(Chapter 14)*

4 Blanche Ingram *(Chapter 17)*

5 Mr Rochester *(Chapter 15)*

6 Jane *(Chapter 23)*

7 Mr Rochester *(Chapter 13)*

8 Blanche Ingram *(Chapter 18)*

9 Bertha Rochester *(Chapter 26)*

TEST YOURSELF (CHAPTERS 28–35)

1 Jane *(Chapter 28)*

2 Diana Rivers *(Chapter 29)*

3 Jane *(Chapter 29)*

4 St John Rivers *(Chapter 30)*

5 St John *(Chapter 33)*

6 St John *(Chapter 32)*

7 Rosamund Oliver *(Chapter 32)*

8 Jane *(Chapter 34)*

TEST YOURSELF (CHAPTERS 36–38)

1 Jane *(Chapter 36)*

2 Jane *(Chapter 37)*

3 Rochester *(Chapter 37)*

4 Rochester *(Chapter 37)*

5 Bertha *(Chapter 36)*

6 Rochester *(Chapter 37)*

7 St John *(Chapter 37)*

NOTES

Maya Angelou
I Know Why the Caged Bird Sings

Jane Austen
Pride and Prejudice

Alan Ayckbourn
Absent Friends

Elizabeth Barrett Browning
Selected Poems

Robert Bolt
A Man for All Seasons

Harold Brighouse
Hobson's Choice

Charlotte Brontë
Jane Eyre

Emily Brontë
Wuthering Heights

Shelagh Delaney
A Taste of Honey

Charles Dickens
David Copperfield
Great Expectations
Hard Times
Oliver Twist

Roddy Doyle
Paddy Clarke Ha Ha Ha

George Eliot
Silas Marner
The Mill on the Floss

Anne Frank
The Diary of a Young Girl

William Golding
Lord of the Flies

Oliver Goldsmith
She Stoops to Conquer

Willis Hall
The Long and the Short and the Tall

Thomas Hardy
Far from the Madding Crowd

The Mayor of Casterbridge
Tess of the d'Urbervilles
The Withered Arm and other Wessex Tales

L.P. Hartley
The Go-Between

Seamus Heaney
Selected Poems

Susan Hill
I'm the King of the Castle

Barry Hines
A Kestrel for a Knave

Louise Lawrence
Children of the Dust

Harper Lee
To Kill a Mockingbird

Laurie Lee
Cider with Rosie

Arthur Miller
The Crucible
A View from the Bridge

Robert O'Brien
Z for Zachariah

Frank O'Connor
My Oedipus Complex and Other Stories

George Orwell
Animal Farm

J.B. Priestley
An Inspector Calls
When We Are Married

Willy Russell
Educating Rita
Our Day Out

J.D. Salinger
The Catcher in the Rye

William Shakespeare
Henry IV Part I
Henry V
Julius Caesar

Macbeth
The Merchant of Venice
A Midsummer Night's Dream
Much Ado About Nothing
Romeo and Juliet
The Tempest
Twelfth Night

George Bernard Shaw
Pygmalion

Mary Shelley
Frankenstein

R.C. Sherriff
Journey's End

Rukshana Smith
Salt on the snow

John Steinbeck
Of Mice and Men

Robert Louis Stevenson
Dr Jekyll and Mr Hyde

Jonathan Swift
Gulliver's Travels

Robert Swindells
Daz 4 Zoe

Mildred D. Taylor
Roll of Thunder, Hear My Cry

Mark Twain
Huckleberry Finn

James Watson
Talking in Whispers

Edith Wharton
Ethan Frome

William Wordsworth
Selected Poems

A Choice of Poets

Mystery Stories of the Nineteenth Century including The Signalman

Nineteenth Century Short Stories

Poetry of the First World War

Six Women Poets

Margaret Atwood
Cat's Eye
The Handmaid's Tale

Jane Austen
Emma
Mansfield Park
Persuasion
Pride and Prejudice
Sense and Sensibility

Alan Bennett
Talking Heads

William Blake
Songs of Innocence and of Experience

Charlotte Brontë
Jane Eyre
Villette

Emily Brontë
Wuthering Heights

Angela Carter
Nights at the Circus

Geoffrey Chaucer
The Franklin's Prologue and Tale
The Miller's Prologue and Tale
The Prologue to the Canterbury Tales
The Wife of Bath's Prologue and Tale

Samuel Coleridge
Selected Poems

Joseph Conrad
Heart of Darkness

Daniel Defoe
Moll Flanders

Charles Dickens
Bleak House
Great Expectations
Hard Times

Emily Dickinson
Selected Poems

John Donne
Selected Poems

Carol Ann Duffy
Selected Poems

George Eliot
Middlemarch
The Mill on the Floss

T.S. Eliot
Selected Poems
The Waste Land

F. Scott Fitzgerald
The Great Gatsby

E.M. Forster
A Passage to India

Brian Friel
Translations

Thomas Hardy
Jude the Obscure
The Mayor of Casterbridge
The Return of the Native
Selected Poems
Tess of the d'Urbervilles

Seamus Heaney
Selected Poems from 'Opened Ground'

Nathaniel Hawthorne
The Scarlet Letter

Homer
The Iliad
The Odyssey

Aldous Huxley
Brave New World

Kazuo Ishiguro
The Remains of the Day

Ben Jonson
The Alchemist

James Joyce
Dubliners

John Keats
Selected Poems

Christopher Marlowe
Doctor Faustus
Edward II

Arthur Miller
Death of a Salesman

John Milton
Paradise Lost Books I & II

Toni Morrison
Beloved

George Orwell
Nineteen Eighty-Four

Sylvia Plath
Selected Poems

Alexander Pope
Rape of the Lock & Selected Poems

William Shakespeare
Antony and Cleopatra
As You Like It
Hamlet
Henry IV Part I
King Lear
Macbeth
Measure for Measure
The Merchant of Venice
A Midsummer Night's Dream
Much Ado About Nothing
Othello
Richard II
Richard III
Romeo and Juliet
The Taming of the Shrew
The Tempest
Twelfth Night
The Winter's Tale

George Bernard Shaw
Saint Joan

Mary Shelley
Frankenstein

Jonathan Swift
Gulliver's Travels and A Modest Proposal

Alfred Tennyson
Selected Poems

Virgil
The Aeneid

Alice Walker
The Color Purple

Oscar Wilde
The Importance of Being Earnest

Tennessee Williams
A Streetcar Named Desire

Jeanette Winterson
Oranges Are Not the Only Fruit

John Webster
The Duchess of Malfi

Virginia Woolf
To the Lighthouse

W.B. Yeats
Selected Poems

Metaphysical Poets

THE ULTIMATE WEB SITE FOR THE ULTIMATE LITERATURE GUIDES

At York Notes we believe in helping you achieve exam success. Log on to **www.yorknotes.com** and see how we have made revision even easier, with over 300 titles available to download twenty-four hours a day. The downloads have lots of additional features such as pop-up boxes providing instant glossary definitions, user-friendly links to every part of the guide, and scanned illustrations offering visual appeal. All you need to do is log on to **www.yorknotes.com** and download the books you need to help you achieve exam success.

KEY FEATURES:

Details on how York Notes can help you

Menu Bar to help you find your way around the site

Details on how to download York Notes

Quick Search facility to help you find the titles you need

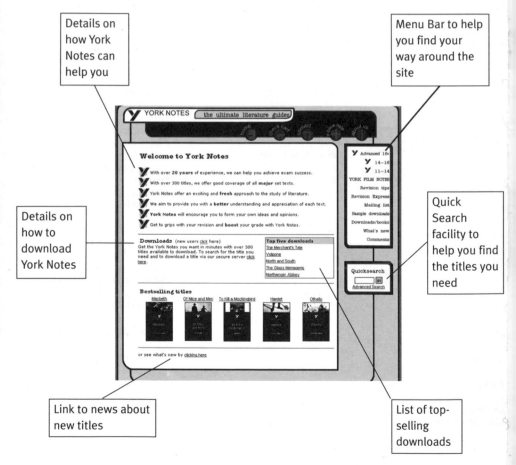

Link to news about new titles

List of top-selling downloads